WJEC/Eduqas **GCSE**

Music

Revision Guide

Jan Richards

Published in 2018 by Illuminate Publishing Ltd,
PO Box 1160, Cheltenham, Gloucestershire GL50 9RW

Orders: Please visit www.illuminatepublishing.com
or email sales@illuminatepublishing.com

British Library Cataloguing-in-Publication Data

A catalogue record for this book is available from the British Library ISBN 978-1-911208-41-9

Printed in England by: Barley Print, Hertfordshire

5.18

The publisher's policy is to use papers that are natural, renewable and recyclable
products made from wood grown in sustainable forests. The logging and manufacturing
processes are expected to conform to the environmental regulations of the country of origin.

Every effort has been made to contact copyright holders of material reproduced in this book.
If notified, the publishers will be pleased to rectify any errors or omissions at the earliest
opportunity.

Editor: Dawn Booth
Text design and layout: kamaedesign
Typeset by York Publishing Solutions Pvt Ltd, India
Cover photograph: © C12 / Alamy Stock Photo

Music acknowledgements

'Handbags and Gladrags' Words and Music by Mike D'Abo © 1968, Reproduced by permission of
EMI United Partnership Ltd, London W1F 9LD.

Light of of the World; (From the musical play Godspell); Words and Music by Stephen Schwartz;
© 1971 RANGE ROAD MUSIC, INC., QUARTET MUSIC, INC., and NEW CADENZA MUSIC CORP. All Rights
Reserved. CARLIN MUSIC CORP., Iron Bridge House, 3 Bridge Approach, Chalk Farm, London, NW1
8BD for the Commonwealth of Nations (excluding Canada/Australia and New Zealand) and Eire.

Since You've Been Gone; Words & Music by Russ Ballard; © Copyright 1976 Russell Ballard Limited.
Union Square Music Songs Limited, A BMG Company. All Rights Reserved. International Copyright
Secured. Used by permission of Music Sales Limited.

Photo acknowledgements

p.1 © C12 / Alamy Stock Photo; p.14 Angelika Smile; p.26 Minerva Studio; p.37 senticus; p.48
Hquality; p.87 Monkey Business Images; p.94 (left) Six Dun; p.94 (right) Ape Man

This book has an accompanying website, at www.illuminate.digital/gcsemusicrevision, where
you can look at and listen to many of the music examples that are shown in it. There are also
links to the web pages that take you to the preferred online music performances you need to
listen to in order to complete the Activities and Exam-style questions.

The login details you need to access this site are:
Username: Illuminatemusicrevise
Password: ComposerRevise

CONTENTS

INTRODUCTION

This GCSE Music revision guide is intended to complement the GCSE Music textbook, and is to be used alongside the information and support given by your teacher.

It contains the necessary information that you need to know and learn when studying the GCSE course in Music. It is not a teaching guide, but it is a useful support for you to refer to and use, outlining essential information and musical knowledge, with guidance on how to answer certain types of question in the Appraising examination.

How will I be assessed?

Performing	Composing	Appraising
Eduqas: 30%	Eduqas: 30%	Eduqas: 40%
WJEC: 35%	WJEC: 35%	WJEC: 30%
• Coursework • Minimum of two pieces • One must be an ensemble • Recorded and assessed by your teacher • Marks will be checked by a moderator from the exam board • WJEC – includes writing a programme note	• Coursework • Two compositions • One must be in response to a set brief • Assessed by your teacher • Marks will be checked by a moderator from the exam board • WJEC – includes writing an evaluation of the piece written to the set brief	• Written examination • Recorded extracts on the four areas of study • Eight questions – two on each area of study • Two of the questions (1 and 7) are based on the prepared extracts set for study • Marked by an examiner from the exam board

The main focus for this revision guide is the listening and appraising component as this is the area where a revision guide can help you most.

The book has been divided into two sections.

Section 1 Appraising

Chapter 1: The elements of music – to highlight their meaning and reinforce your understanding

Chapter 2: Prepared extracts Eduqas

Chapter 3: Prepared extracts WJEC

(The above chapters reinforce the main features of the prepared extracts, approached through each of the musical elements in turn.)

Chapter 4: Aural dictation – includes exercises for you to improve your aural, reading and writing skills in music

Chapter 5: Exam-style questions – answers and commentaries; looks at the different types of questions and offers suggestions on exam technique

Chapter 6: Musical terms and theory – lists all the terminology you need to be familiar with for assessment

Section 2 Composing and performing

This section reminds you of the requirements of the examination and outlines approaches that will support you in the preparation of your coursework.

Chapter 7: Composing

Chapter 8: Performing

What do I need to know?

There are four areas of study that need to be covered throughout the course:

Area of study 1 Musical forms and devices

Area of study 2 Music for ensemble

Area of study 3 Film music

Area of study 4 Popular music

During your study of these topics, you will need to consider the **musical elements**, **musical contexts** and **musical language**.

You will be exploring a wide variety of music, for sure.

How to use this revision guide

This revision guide contains a range of features to help you learn and revise.

Key terms provide definitions of all the essential musical terminology you will be expected to know for assessment.

Get the grade offers suggestions on how to maximise marks.

BOOK LINK **Book link** references relevant pages from the student book to make it easier for you to refer back to the student book for more in-depth information.

Revision tip provides help and advice on ways to help you prepare for assessment.

Remember highlights important things that you need to know.

Activity 1.1 **Activities** suggested throughout the guide provide opportunities for you to practise applying your musical knowledge (AO3) and using your appraising skills to make evaluative and critical judgements about music (AO4). When you see this symbol it means that you need to *look* at the music extracts and answer the related questions. This symbol means you need to *listen* to the extracts, which are available online, and answer the linked questions. These *looking* and *listening* skills are really important skills that you need to practise.

Wherever you see this symbol you can go to the accompanying website for this book (www.illuminate.digital/gcsemusicrevision) and you will find the associated musical extract or a link to the relevant online clips. You can access the book's website with the following Username and Password:

Username: Illuminatemusicrevise
Password: ComposerRevise

How can I revise for the Appraising examination?

Your musical skills and understanding will build up throughout the course. However, there are things that must be learned, and it is always advisable not to leave things until the last minute. Make sure you learn the pitch names of all notes, the rhythmic note-values, the key signatures and time signatures, the terminology, and the musical signs. The detailed information that you will have been taught on the prepared extracts is a must to learn.

Examination technique is the final factor in ensuring success. Make sure that you complete plenty of practice questions in the style of the examination. Your teacher will go over examples in class with you, and outline hints and tips on the best way to answer. Many students will focus on what marks they achieve in such practice questions – but the really important thing to remember is to remain patient and concentrate when correcting them. If you score well, it is only too easy to quickly dismiss what was incorrect; the secret is to fully appreciate why something was marked as being wrong ... and what observations or details you should have included to get a better result.

What can I do to help myself?

- Broaden your knowledge and understanding by listening to a wide variety of music linked to the areas of study.
- Visit relevant websites that will support your understanding further.
- Use specific subject vocabulary to ensure your use of terminology is accurate.
- Completing typical examination questions will improve your skills as you become ever more familiar with what is required.
- When composing, work regularly and steadily on your ideas, plan the content carefully and be prepared to accept constructive advice from your teacher.
- Be organised!
- Set challenges and targets for yourself; make sure that you know what is expected of you and work diligently to reach your potential.
- In terms of the performing – practise, practise, practise! Embrace the challenge of performing in front of others and with others to improve your confidence.

Good luck!

SECTION 1
APPRAISING

CHAPTER 1: THE ELEMENTS OF MUSIC

What Do I Need To Know?

This section is intended to remind you of the basic information about the elements of music. You need to remember:

▶ that you have to apply the elements of music to every area of study

▶ that your answers in the Appraising paper must focus on recognising and understanding the elements of music

▶ that the performance of your selected pieces must reflect an understanding of the required musical elements (such as dynamics, tempo and rhythm)

▶ that your compositions must demonstrate technical control of the musical elements.

These are the musical elements:

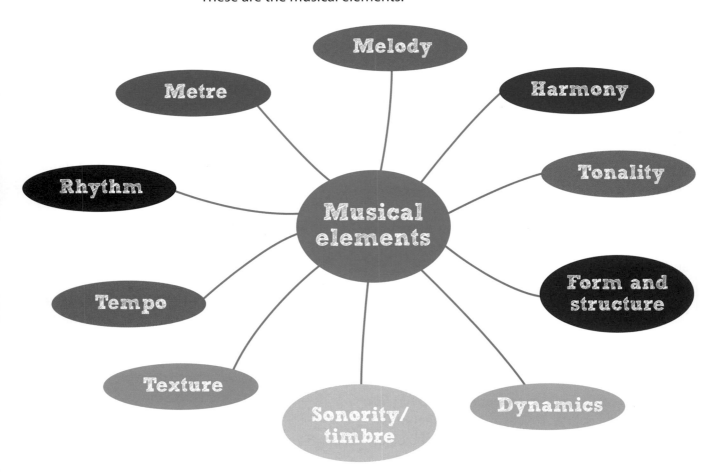

Pitch

When we talk about the 'pitch' in music, we are thinking about whether the music is high or low – or in between. It is the different position of the different sounds which are the musical notes. In this respect, you need to think about:

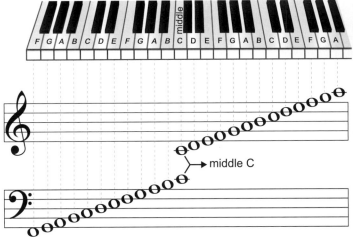

- the melody and its range
- what intervals may be included
- what patterns or devices may be used
- how contrast is achieved.

The pitch is identified through the musical notes, where they are placed on the **stave** and identified by the **clefs** that are used.

 Key terms

Stave
Sometimes called the staff. The name given to the five lines and four spaces that music is written on.

Clef
The symbol at the start of the musical line. The clefs you need to know are the **treble** clef (used for higher-pitched voices and instruments) and the **bass** clef (used for lower-pitched voices and instruments).

The distance between two musical notes is known as an **interval**. There are different types of intervals: some are small (because the notes are close together) and others are large (because the notes are further apart). The most common way of organising the pitches in music can be understood by learning about the musical **scales**, of which there are also different types.

You must learn the names of the treble and bass clef notes, and be aware of the musical movement in a melody – both in written notation and when listening to extracts in the appraising examination.

☑ **Get the Grade**

You will also need to know about the **viola** clef (or **alto** clef as it is sometimes called) for the more in-depth analysis of the prepared extracts you must study.

 Remember

Some of the different types of scales are:
- Major scales
- Minor scales
- Chromatic scales
- Pentatonic scales
- Blues scales

Activity 1.1

Here are some **pitch** exercises to get you started.

A The following 12 musical patterns each consist of five notes. In each pattern, identify:
- Which written note would be the 'highest' pitch?
- Which written note would be the 'lowest' pitch?
- Which written note would give the 'middle' pitch in each pattern?

 Try completing this task without listening to the extracts at first.

 Now play each of the patterns on a keyboard (or any instrument of your choice), or listen to the extracts to check your answers and hear how they sound.

 B Now listen to extracts 1–10, all of which contain four musical pitches or notes.

- Which note in each pattern is the highest-pitched sound – 1, 2, 3 or 4?

- Which note in each pattern is the lowest-pitched sound – 1, 2, 3 or 4?

 C One of the questions in the Appraising examination will require you to add the missing pitch in a given melody. Here are some examples for you to try.

The rhythm has been given – complete the melody by filling in the missing notes.

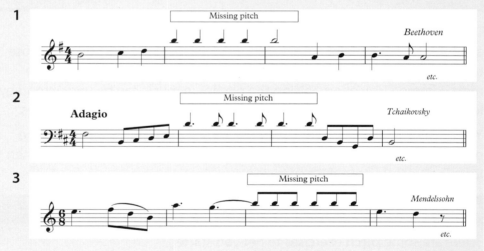

Rhythm

When we talk about the 'rhythm' of the music, we are thinking about the patterns of the long and short notes used within the strong and weak beats. You need to know and understand the note-values (e.g. semibreve, minim, quaver, etc.) and how rhythmic devices are used (e.g. dotted rhythms, syncopation, triplets, rests, tied notes, etc.).

◀ The rhythm tree

Metre

The metre is the repeating pattern of strong beats and weak beats that give us the pulse in the music. It is shown in the score by the use of the **time signature**. There are two different types of time signature – **simple time** and **compound time**. For GCSE Music, you must learn about the time signatures as shown in the diagram on the right.

SIMPLE TIME		
2/4	3/4	4/4
COMPOUND TIME		
6/8		

Simple time is when the pulse of the music can be broken down and identified as two 'inner' beats. In the time signatures you need to know, the type of beat is a crotchet beat.

2/4 = 2 crotchet beats in a bar (e.g. ♩♩ or ♫ ♫)

3/4 = 3 crotchet beats in a bar (e.g. ♩♩♩ or ♫ ♫ ♫)

4/4 = 4 crotchet beats in a bar (e.g. ♩♩♩♩ or ♫ ♫ ♫ ♫)

Key terms

Simple time
Counts crotchet beats in every bar.

Compound time
Counts dotted crotchet beats per bar.

Compound time is when the pulse of the music can be broken down and identified as three 'inner' beats. This type of beat is a dotted crotchet beat.

You may think that this should feel as if there are six beats in a bar, but it actually feels like two strong beats, each with an underlying feel of three 'inner beats'.

6/8 = 2 dotted crotchet beats in bar (e.g. ♩. ♩. and ♫♫♫ 1 2 3 4 5 6)

Learn and understand these time signatures to recognise where the strong accents are and whether the beat feels regular or irregular.

The **tempo** is the speed of the beat. Make sure you know about the different speeds and the Italian terminology (e.g. allegro, largo, rallentando, etc.).

More information on these terms may be found in Chapter 6.

Remember
Another word for the 'beat' is the 'pulse'.

Activity 1.2

Here are some **rhythm** exercises to get you started.

A The following rhythmic patterns consist of various different note-values. In each pattern, identify:
- Which written note would sound the shortest when performed?
- Which written note would sound the longest when performed?

B Can you tell the difference between simple time and compound time?

Listen to the opening part of the following five extracts and underline the correct answer.

Extract 1 • Dvořák: 'Scherzo' from *Serenade for Strings*, Op. 22	Simple time / Compound time
Extract 2 • Beethoven: *Piano Sonata,* Op. 31 No. 3, Menuetto	Simple time / Compound time
Extract 3 • Handel: 'O, Lovely Peace' from *Judas Maccabeus*	Simple time / Compound time
Extract 4 • Schubert: *Symphony No. 9 in C major*, movement 1	Simple time / Compound time
Extract 5 • Grieg: 'Morning' from *Peer Gynt*	Simple time / Compound time

 C Now listen to extracts 1–4 and tap or play the rhythm as you listen to the music. They are in different time signatures and include some rests.

Extract 1

Extract 2

Extract 3

Extract 4

D One of the questions in the Appraising examination may require you to identify the correct rhythmic pattern played in the extract. Let's try it.

1 Listen to the following musical phrase.

Dvořák: *Symphony No. 9 in E minor*

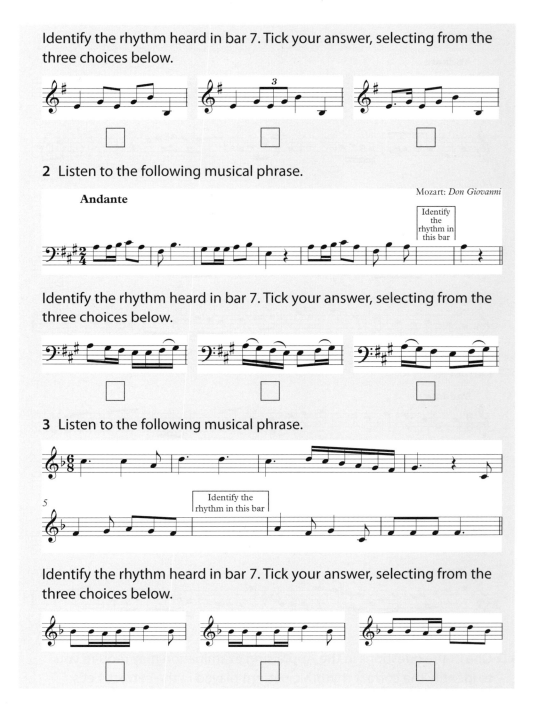

Identify the rhythm heard in bar 7. Tick your answer, selecting from the three choices below.

2 Listen to the following musical phrase.

Andante

Mozart: *Don Giovanni*

Identify the rhythm in this bar

Identify the rhythm heard in bar 7. Tick your answer, selecting from the three choices below.

3 Listen to the following musical phrase.

Identify the rhythm in this bar

Identify the rhythm heard in bar 7. Tick your answer, selecting from the three choices below.

Melody

A melody is a series of pitches heard in succession; it's a line of musical notes that is satisfying to listen to. The melody may also be referred to as the 'tune' or sometimes the 'theme'.

▶ 'Variations on a Theme of Paganini', by Brahms, is an example of a well-known melody.

Melody is a combination of pitch and rhythm. It may incorporate such **musical devices** as repetition, sequence, imitation, contrast, call and response, fanfare ideas, and decorations or **embellishments**. It may use stepwise movement (i.e. scalic or conjunct movement), jumpy movement (i.e using intervals or disjunct movement) – or a combination of both.

Definitions of **musical devices** can be found in Chapter 6.

> **Key term**
>
> **Embellishment**
> A decorative musical detail or feature that makes the music more interesting.

Activity 1.3

Here are some exercises on **melody**.

A Can you tell the difference between conjunct and disjunct movement?

By looking at the following extracts, decide whether you think the melody is mainly conjunct or disjunct. Underline your answer.

1	Conjunct / Disjunct
2	Conjunct / Disjunct
3	Conjunct / Disjunct
4	Conjunct / Disjunct

Extension questions:

- Can you tap out the rhythms of these phrases?
- Can you play them on an instrument of your choice?
- Listen to the extracts online – do you think they are in major or minor keys?

B Now look at, and also listen to, the following extracts. Identify the melodic device (or devices) used in each.

Extract 1

Extract 2

Extract 3

Extract 4

Harmony

Harmony is a combination of notes played at the same time. The harmony in the music supports the melody, reinforces the rhythmic movement and also provides interest in its own right. Music may use diatonic, chromatic or dissonant harmony.

- **Diatonic harmony** is when the music uses chords based on major or minor keys.
- **Chromatic harmony** is when extra sharps or flats are added to the chords – notes not in the key of the piece – making it sound richer and more complex.
- **Dissonant harmony** uses notes that do not belong to any key as such – as a result it may sound quite harsh and be 'clashy' sounding.

You need to know about primary and secondary chords, cadences and devices such as 'drones', 'pedal' notes and 'power chords' (found in rock and pop music). You must also make sure that you understand all the harmonies, chords and cadences in the prepared extracts selected for study.

Definitions for 'drones', 'pedal' and 'power chords' can be found in Chapter 6.

Activity 1.4

Here are some exercises on **harmony**.

 A Music teachers often describe 'major' chords as sounding 'happy', and 'minor' chords as sounding 'sad'.

Listen to the following ten chords and decide whether you think they are major or minor.

	Major or minor?		**Major or minor?**
Chord 1 ▶		Chord 2 ▶	
Chord 3 ▶		Chord 4 ▶	
Chord 5 ▶		Chord 6 ▶	
Chord 7 ▶		Chord 8 ▶	
Chord 9 ▶		Chord 10 ▶	

B In each of the following six examples, identify the type of harmony that is being heard. Tick the correct answer from the three choices given.

	Diatonic	Chromatic	Dissonant
Extract 1			
Extract 2			
Extract 3			
Extract 4			
Extract 5			
Extract 6			

Tonality

When we talk about tonality, we generally mean the **key** of the music. This is what helps define the character of a piece. In fact, it usually refers to the whole system of tonal relationships between the notes, the chords and the key of the music. It is occasionally called major–minor tonality, as it depends on the major and minor scales and what chords are possible using notes from those scales. So, to establish the key of a piece, you must check the key signature at the start of the score.

Sometimes the music **modulates** (i.e. changes key). For this examination, you need to know the key signatures of major and minor keys up to four sharps and four flats. You must understand about modulation to the dominant key, and modulation to the relative major/minor key.

You must also understand what is meant by **pentatonic** tonality.

The pentatonic scale can actually feel 'major' or 'minor' – which may seem very confusing. However, it does have a very particular and distinctive musical 'flavour' of its own, and may be heard in many examples of folk music (e.g. Scottish and Appalachian folk music) and in oriental music (e.g. Chinese music). It is also used a lot in rock music. Many tunes in this genre are pentatonic, although the accompaniments may well be more adventurous. Interesting clips to watch may be found online.

⭐ **Revision tip**

We say a piece of music is ATONAL when there is **no** sense of key or major–minor relationship evident in the music. Please note: knowledge of this is **not** required in the Eduqas/WJEC GCSE Music specification.

⭐ **Revision tip**

When trying to establish the tonality of a piece of music, try to get a feel of the 'overall' key – don't listen to individual chords. A piece of music in a major key will use some minor chords, and a piece of music in a minor key will use some major chords. However, it is a good idea to get the 'feel' of a key by concentrating on chords at the very start and also at the very end of a piece or section of the music.

Overall, does it feel 'happy' (i.e. major) or 'sad' (i.e. minor)?

Activity 1.5

Here are some exercises on tonality.

 A Major, minor or pentatonic? Listen to the following five extracts and underline the correct description of the harmony.

Extract 1 ▶	Major / Minor / Pentatonic
Extract 2 ▶	Major / Minor / Pentatonic
Extract 3 ▶	Major / Minor / Pentatonic
Extract 4 ▶	Major / Minor / Pentatonic
Extract 5 ▶	Major / Minor / Pentatonic

 B Listen to the following four extracts, and decide which of the comments best describes the tonality. Tick the correct answer. You have been given the melody line in each case.

	Major key through-out	Minor key through-out	Modulates major → minor	Modulates minor → major
Extract 1 ▶				
Extract 2 ▶				
Extract 3 ▶				
Extract 4 ▶				

Form and structure

Structure plays such an important part in music; it is what gives the content shape and balance. For example, the structure of a melody may depend on stepwise or scalic patterns (i.e. conjunct movement), more angular ideas (i.e. disjunct movement) or patterns using the notes of a triad (such as a fanfare). It may be a mix of all three – and it then depends on how the musical ideas and patterns have been organised into motifs, melodies and themes, and how they are used and presented. They could be repeated, contrasted and developed in many different ways.

Form in music is the name given to the overall structure in a piece of music, according to how all the ideas have been organised to create the finished piece. For identification purposes, each section in the music is usually labelled with a capital letter: A, B, C and so on.

You will come across many different forms in the four areas of study, including:

- binary form
- ternary form
- rondo form
- minuet and trio form
- strophic form
- theme and variations form
- 32-bar song form
- 12-bar blues.

You will need to demonstrate your understanding of form and structure in composing, and explain the details of your work in the candidate log. You will also be required to identify structural features and devices of the music when responding to musical extracts in the listening examination.

The most challenging questions on form will be on the various prepared extracts, as these are complete pieces which you have studied in more depth.

Activity 1.6

Here are some questions on **structure**.

A Draw a line to match the forms to the letters that suggest the overall structure.

Binary form	A B A C A
Strophic form	A B A
Rondo form	A A B A
32-bar song form	A B
Ternary form	A B A B A B etc.

B Are the following statements about structure true or false? Underline the correct answer.

1	In binary form, both sections are usually in the same key.	True / False
2	In ternary form, the third section is based on the first.	True / False
3	Rondo form consists of five contrasting sections.	True / False
4	In binary form, the beginning of section B is usually in a related key.	True / False
5	In ternary form, the second section is always in a different time signature than the first section.	True / False
6	Rondo form uses a recurring section that is based on the opening material.	True / False

Dynamics

The dynamic markings in a piece of music instruct the performers how loud or quiet to play. So, it is important to know what the terms and signs mean.

ppp pp p mp mf f ff fff
Softest.. Loudest

These dynamic markings are placed underneath the musical stave.

Other important terminology may be found in Chapter 6.

Activity 1.7

 A Using the information above, look at the melody below and answer the following questions:

1 Which note will sound the loudest?

2 Which note will sound the quietest?

3 In which bars will the music gradually be getting louder?

4 In which bars will the music gradually be getting quieter?

 Get the Grade

Some useful terms:
Crescendo means 'getting louder' (sometimes abbreviated to 'cresc.').

Decrescendo means 'getting quieter' (sometimes abbreviated to 'decresc.').

Diminuendo also means 'getting quieter' (sometimes abbreviated to 'dim.').

 Revision tip

As you listen to (and perform) various types of music while studying the GCSE Music course, try to identify what the dynamics of a piece, or part of a piece, should be, so you get used to using the terminology.

Make sure you add some dynamics into your own composition, so that it sounds interesting.

THE ELEMENTS OF MUSIC

Sonority / Timbre

This element is all about the quality of the sounds that we hear in music. In the current GCSE Music specification, it refers to:

- different instruments, types of voices and types of groupings (i.e. what is playing or singing)

- the use of technology (i.e. what is being used and how)

- any performance techniques and articulation (i.e. how the instruments and/ or voices are being used).

Activity 1.8

Here are some revision questions on voices and types of instrumentation and technology for you to try.

Instruments

1 What is the name of the smallest woodwind instrument?

2 Can you name three different keyboard instruments?

3 What are the names of the instruments played with a double reed?

4 What is used to change the tone on a brass instrument?

5 How many families of instruments are there in an orchestra? Name them.

6 How is the musical sound produced on a flute?

7 Why is the harp different from the other string instruments?

8 What is an 'open note' on a string instrument?

9 How many strings are there usually on a bass guitar?

10 What is the difference between a wind band and an orchestra?

11 What is the name given to the group that has two violins, a viola and a violoncello?

12 What does pizzicato mean?

13 What is the difference between tuned and untuned percussion instruments?

14 Give another name for kettledrums.

15 What is a rim-shot?

Voices

1 What is the highest type of female singing voice?

2 What is the lowest male singing voice?

3 What would the letters S.A.T.B. stand for on a piece of choral music?

4 What is the difference between a tenor and a baritone?

5 What is the difference between a soprano and a contralto?

6 What is a mezzo-soprano?

7 What is the term used to describe vocal music without instrumental accompaniment?

8 What is the vocal technique used when singers close their mouths to make the sounds?

9 What technique is used by male singers to sing higher than their normal vocal range?

10 What is the name given to the vocal style that relies on rhythmic delivery of the words in popular music?

11 What is it called when a singer uses different notes to sing one syllable of the text?

12 Name the type of jazz vocal style where the singer relies on delivering sounds rather than words to perform.

13 What description is given to the cast of singers in a musical or opera?

14 What is the term for the musical vocal setting in which every syllable of the text is given a separate pitch or note?

15 What type of choir would include parts for tenors, baritones and basses?

Technology

1 What does MIDI stand for?

2 What is the name given to the electronic keyboard instrument that is able to generate many different types of timbres?

3 What is the name of the device used to alter the sound of amplified electronic instruments?

4 What is meant by reverb?

5 What is a 'sampler' (often used in music technology)?

6 Feedback is caused by the output of the speaker systems being picked up and re-amplified creating a kind of 'loop' effect'. True or false?

7 A wah-wah pedal is used with drum kits. True or false?

8 What is a tremolo arm?

9 What is a tremolo effect?

10 What is the name given to the practice of balancing the sound between two speakers?

Texture

The texture of the music is much more than whether the music feels 'thin' or 'thick'. It refers to the way that the melody and chords have been woven together to achieve different effects – the layers of music and how they relate to each other. Make sure you are able to identify the following textures:

Type of texture	Explanation	
Monophonic	A single melodic line, with no harmonies or other melodies.	**Monophonic**
Homophonic	A chordal style; melody plus chords, sometimes providing a rhythmic contrast.	**Homophonic**
Polyphonic	More than one part delivering the melody (or melodies) in imitation or in counterpoint.	**Polyphonic**

Activity 1.9

Here are some exercises on **texture**.

A Listen to the opening part of the extracts online. State whether you think the texture is monophonic, homophonic or polyphonic.

Extract 1 ▶	_____phonic
Extract 2 ▶	_____phonic
Extract 3 ▶	_____phonic
Extract 4 ▶	_____phonic
Extract 5 ▶	_____phonic
Extract 6 ▶	_____phonic

 B With some friends, listen to the 'Hallelujah Chorus' from the oratorio *Messiah* by G.F. Handel, a composer from the Baroque era in music. You will actually be able to read the music as you listen, by finding the score on the International Music Score Library Project (IMSLP).

Task

Discuss the texture found in the music, to appreciate how different types of texture may be used in the same piece.

 ### Extended listening

'Scherzo' from Schubert's *Piano Sonata in B major D.575*: from the start to 1'06".

Task

Identify the different types of texture used in the 'Scherzo' movement by Schubert.

Exam-style questions

 Remember

The following exam questions have been linked to different exams, either Eduqas or WJEC. However, the questions are all on musical elements, so will be useful practice for students following either syllabus.

 Bach, *Minuet in G*   **[WJEC: 9 marks]**

You will hear a performance of the first part of a piece by J.S. Bach. Play the extract four times. The melody is printed below.

(a) (i) Identify the correct bars played by the bass line in bars 9 and 10. Tick the correct answer from the three choices below.   **[1 mark]**

(ii) Name the cadence heard in bars 7^3–8.   **[1 mark]**

....

(iii) Name the musical device used in bars 13–15.   **[1 mark]**

....

(iv) Complete the missing notes of the melody in bars 3–4. (You will see that the rhythm is given for you.)   **[3 marks]**

(b) Give the full name of the key of the extract (e.g. B♭ major). **[1 mark]**

....

(c) Identify the instrument playing in this extract. **[1 mark]**

....

(d) Suggest a tempo marking for this extract (e.g. allegro). **[1 mark]**

....

Film theme, *Laurence of Arabia* (from the start to 1'08") **[Eduqas 12 marks]**

You will hear an extract of film music, played from the start. It is about a man who led the Arabian tribes with the British army in its fight against the Turks.

Listen to it **three** times.

(a) The instruments heard at the beginning of this extract are from the PERCUSSION family. Name two of the percussion instruments heard in the first part of the extract.

  (i) .... **[1 mark]**

  (ii) .... **[1 mark]**

(b) Describe how the composer creates the required mood and atmosphere in this extract. In your answer you must refer to:

- the musical elements
- the purpose and intention of the music. **[10 marks]**

(This is a longer answer question and about two pages would be provided in the answer booklet in an examination. If you want to attempt this answer you will need to use separate sheets of paper.)

Beatles, 'Yesterday' (from the start to 1'00") **[WJEC 9 marks]**

Listen to the first two verses of **Version 1** of this song. Then answer the following questions.

(a) Two of the following statements are true. Tick the two statements that you believe to be true. **[2 marks]**

Statement	Tick
The introduction is played on a percussion instrument.	
The introduction is two bars long.	
This song is sung by a bass singer.	
A string accompaniment is added in verse two.	

Now listen to another two versions of '**Yesterday**':

'Yesterday' Version 2 (from the start to 1'16")

(b) Note three ways in which **Version 2** is different from the original (**Version 1**). **[3 marks]**

  (i) ....

  (ii) ....

  (iii) ....

'Yesterday' Version 3 (from the start to 1'17")

(c) Note three ways in which **Version 3** is different from the original (**Version 1**).　　**[3 marks]**

(i) ....

(ii) ....

(iii) ....

Version 3

(d) Tick the box that correctly identifies the type of instruments performing in **Version 3**. **[1 mark]**

Violins	**Violas**	**Cellos**	**Double basses**
☐	☐	☐	☐

'O Chan Mere Makna' (from the start to 1'20")　　　　**[Eduqas 12 marks]**

You will hear an extract from a song called '**O Chan Mere Makna**'.

Play the song four times. (In the exam you would have 30 seconds to read the questions before the first playing of the extract. Then it would be played four times with a 30-second pause between each playing, and a three-minute silence after the final playing for you to complete your answer.)

(a) Underline the term which best describes the opening of the extract.　　**[1 mark]**

Unaccompanied　　　　**Homophonic**　　　　**Imitative**

(b) Underline the most suitable **tempo** marking for this piece of music.　　**[1 mark]**

Largo　　　　**Presto**　　　　**Moderato**

(c) Underline the time signature of the music.　　**[1 mark]**

3/4　　　　**4/4**　　　　**5/4**

(d) Describe the **structure** of the extract, as far as 1'20".　　**[3 marks]**
[One mark per relevant comment.]

....

....

....

(e) Identify three features that can be traced back to the influence of original bhangra music.　　**[3 marks]**

(i) ....

(ii) ....

(iii) ....

(f) Identify two features that have been influenced by contemporary pop/dance music. **[2 marks]**

(i) ....

(ii) ....

(g) Suggest an occasion when this type of music may be performed.　　**[1 mark]**

....

Welsh folk music [WJEC 9 marks]

To complete this question, you must listen to the first part of the track, as far as 1'38".

You will hear an extract of Welsh folk music. Listen to the extract twice. (In the examination the extract will be played twice with a 30-second pause after each playing.)

(a) Name the vocal technique used in the opening section. [1 mark]

....

(b) The extract (until 1'38") presents the first two sections of the overall structure. Identify the sections in the order in which they are heard. [2 marks]

Section 1 ....   Section 2 ....

(c) Listen carefully to the pitch of the first phrase sung by the soloist to the words **'Paham mae dicter, O Myfanwy'**.

Identify the melody by ticking the correct answer from the three choices below. [1 mark]

☐

☐

☐

(d) Underline the correct tonality of the music. [1 mark]

Major   **Minor**   **Pentatonic**

(e) In the table below, tick one musical feature of **tempo** heard in this extract. [1 mark]

Musical feature	Tick
Accelerando	
Rubato	
Allegro	

(f) Complete the following sentences with the correct musical term. [3 marks]

(i) This performance, without an instrumental accompaniment, is known as ....

(ii) The type of choir singing in the extract is a ....

(iii) The texture of the singing in this extract is ....

CHAPTER 2: PREPARED EXTRACTS EDUQAS

What Do I Need To Know?

There are two prepared extracts of music that you must learn in more detail. Each is linked to a different area of study:

▶ *Eine Kleine Nachtmusik*, Minuet and Trio by Mozart (movement 3)

▶ 'Since You've Been Gone' by Rainbow.

In the Appraising examination, the Mozart question will always be question 1. The Rainbow question will always be question 7. Both will be marked out of 12 marks (the same as all the other questions on the paper).

 BOOK LINK: pages 43–47

BOOK LINK: pages 162–206

Prepared extract 1: Mozart, Minuet and Trio (*Eine Kleine Nachtmusik*)

Background details

- The composer was Wolfgang Amadeus Mozart (1756–1791).

- He was considered to be one of the main composers of the Classical era in music.

- This piece was composed in 1787.

- *Eine Kleine Nachtmusik* is German for 'a little serenade' but it has become more commonly known as 'a little night music'.

- This very popular piece was not published until 1827, many years after Mozart's death.

Musical elements

Form and structure

- The Minuet is in binary form.

- The Trio is in binary form.

- The overall plan of this movement is Minuet – Trio – Minuet (just like an A B A structure). It is normal practice to repeat the **Menuetto (da capo)** following the Trio.

- Each section of the piece is eight bars long – and each section is repeated.

- The music is organised into regular four-bar phrases.

- The final phrase in each B section repeats the 2nd phrase of the previous A sections.

🔍 Key term

Menuetto da capo
The instruction 'da capo' (sometimes shortened to DC) instructs performers to play the music again 'from the beginning'. The Minuet is therefore repeated after the Trio.

Minuet		Trio	
Section A	Section B	Section A	Section B
:Bars 1–8 :	:Bars 9–16 :	:Bars 17–24 :	:Bars 25–36 :
Minuet theme is introduced	A contrasting section 2nd 4-bar phrase of B repeats the 2nd 4-bar phrase of A	New, gentle melody	Quaver movement in upper 3 parts before the Trio 'A' melody returns
←————————→	←————————→	←————————→	←————————→
Repeated	Repeated	Repeated	Repeated

Menuetto da capo

Texture

Homophonic: melody and accompaniment. Throughout, the melody is often played by the violins in octaves. At other times the violins are in harmony (in 3rds or 6ths).

Even though the score is written for four parts, ideas are often in three parts (with ideas doubled up in octaves) and sometimes even in two parts (e.g. the opening).

Minuet		Trio	
Section A	Section B	Section A	Section B
:Bars 1–8 :	:Bars 9–16 :	:Bars 17–24 :	:Bars 25–36 :
Homophonic Opening texture is in two parts until b. 4, as violins share the theme (in 8ves) and violas and cellos share the same idea (also in 8ves) B. 5: 4-part harmony	Thinner texture, opens in violins only – feel of a single line of melody with violins still 8ves apart. Fills out by b. 12 with all parts joining, though still has feeling of 3 parts until the final cadence (which is in 4-part harmony) Homophonic to end	Homophonic – melody + accompaniment	Non-thematic material with quavers in top 3 parts to start this section, and the bass supports. Return of theme in b. 29; melody + accompaniment to finish

⭐ **Revision tip**

- In 8ves means 'in octaves'.
- A perfect octave is an interval eight notes apart, e.g. from one 'E' to the next 'E', i.e. eight notes higher.
- B. 4 means bar 4, etc.

Instrumentation

- String chamber ensemble (with an optional part for double bass).
- The score for study has four parts, just like a string quartet: violin 1, violin 2, viola and cello.
- Often performed by a string orchestra.

Tempo

The tempo is allegretto, which means 'moderately fast' (slower than allegro).

Revision tip

Minuet

- The home key, i.e. G major, is also referred to as the **tonic** key.

- The **submediant** is the sixth step of the scale (E is the sixth note of the scale of G major).

- The **dominant** note is the fifth step of the scale (D is the fifth note of the scale of G major).

Trio

- D major is the tonic key of the Trio.

- The dominant note is the fifth step of the scale (A is the fifth note of the scale of D major).

 Revision tip

- The pitch range in each part is quite narrow.

- Melodic ideas include both conjunct and disjunct movement.

- Each section begins with an anacrusis.

- B. 6^2 means the 2nd beat of bar 6, b. 7^1 means the first beat of bar 7, etc.

Dynamics

- Range from **p** (piano – soft) to **f** (forte – loud).

- Minuet: Section A begins forte; Section B begins piano, but goes back to forte by bar 13.

- Trio: Section A melody is sotto voce ('hushed') with piano accompaniment, and the section remains piano throughout.

Rhythm

- Both the Minuet and Trio are in triple time.

- Written as 3/4 (i.e. three crotchet beats in every bar).

- Simple rhythms throughout, using note-values from semiquavers to minims. Lots of quaver movement, with some dotted rhythms in the melody of the Trio.

Tonality

Minuet		Trio	
Section A	Section B	Section A	Section B
:Bars 1–8 :	:Bars 9–16 :	:Bars 17–24 :	:Bars 25–36 :
G major	Starts in E minor (submediant minor) ⇒ D major (dominant major b. 12) ⇒ G major (tonic b. 13)	D major	⇒ A major (dominant major, b. 28) ⇒ D major (tonic, b. 29)

← Repeated → | ← Repeated → | ← Repeated → | ← Repeated →

Melody

Minuet		Trio	
Section A	Section B	Section A	Section B
:Bars 1–8 :	:Bars 9–16 :	:Bars 17–24 :	:Bars 25–36 :
Begins with anacrusis	Begins with anacrusis	Begins with anacrusis	Begins with anacrusis
Opening ascends in crotchets	Opening descends in quavers	Lyrical and gentle melody	Melodic content is conjunct (b. 24–28) except for b. 27^3 – minor 3rds in violin, and a rising dim. 5th in viola
Includes ornaments:	Some ideas are heard as a sequence b. 11–12 is based on b. 9–10, also b. 14–15)	Mainly conjunct (perfect 5th end of b. 19–20 and end of b. 21–22), also some minor 3rds	
Appoggiatura (b. 4^1)			Again use of sequence, e.g. b. 33–34
Trills (b. 6^2 and 7^1)			
Quavers in viola (b. 4)		Accidentals in violin 1 are chromatic stepwise movement, to add colouring and melodic decoration	
Seqential idea in b. 6–7			
		Use of sequence (b. 21–22)	

Harmony

The harmony is described as **diatonic**. In the Appraising examination, you could be asked to describe or identify any chord or key at any point. For revision purposes, this guide identifies the main harmonic features in each section in the following table.

Minuet		Trio	
Section A	Section B	Section A	Section B
:Bars 1–8 :	:Bars 9–16 :	:Bars 17–24 :	:Bars 25–36 :
Mix of root position and first inversion chords Chords change (mostly) on every beat V7 chords B. 3^3 –4 inverted perfect cadence in D (i.e. modulation to dominant key) B. 5–back to G Ends perfect cadence in G (V7–I)	E minor established via diminished 7th chord in 3rd inversion (b. 9^3) D major established via diminished 7th chord in 3rd inversion (b. 11^3) This is a harmonic sequence From b. 13, harmony repeats b. 5–8 Ends perfect cadence in G (V7–I)	Slower rate of chord change (b. 16^3–23) tonic chord D for 2 bars, then dominant A7/A for 2 bars Then one chord per bar: b. 21–D / I B. 22–Bm / vi From b. 23, chord changes quicken to one chord per beat, travelling towards the cadence Ends perfect cadence in D (V7–I)	Starts V of D major (note the inclusion of the 9th in the melody) First phrase ends with a perfect cadence in A major Quick move back to D by b. 29 Remaining harmony = 16^3–24, again with a slower rate of change (i.e. one chord per bar) until the final perfect cadence in D major (V7–I, b. 23–24)

Activity 2.1

Harmony

Try answering these questions about the Mozart extract set for study. They are worth 1 mark each.

1 The chord at the start of bar 1 is:

- ☐ major in root position
- ☐ minor in first inversion
- ☐ major in first inversion
- ☐ minor in root position.

2 The chord in bar 14^1 (i.e. bar 14, first beat) is:

- ☐ a dominant 7th in root position
- ☐ a dominant 7th in first inversion
- ☐ a dominant 7th in second inversion
- ☐ a dominant 7th in third inversion.

 Get the Grade

Use the correct terminology when writing about **melody**:

- **Anacrusis** means 'up-beat'.
- An **appoggiatura** is a decorative 'grace note', which takes half the value of the next note.
- A **trill** is a common musical ornament that involves rapid alternation between one note and the note next to it in pitch, i.e. quick movement between two adjacent notes.
- **Chromatic** movement involves movement to notes that are not in the scale or the given key. A chromatic scale is a musical scale with 12 pitches, each a semitone above or below another.
- A dim. 5th is a diminished 5th, i.e. a perfect 5th that has been made a semitone smaller. In this case, it is the G# to D in the viola part (end of the third bar in the Trio section).

⭐ Revision tip

- D major is the dominant of G – so, at the end of the Trio, the harmony is perfectly placed for a return to the home key of G major.

- In a root position chord, the root note of the triad is played in the bass.

- In a first inversion chord, the 3rd of the triad is heard in the bass.

- Every section ends with a perfect cadence.

3 The chord that supports the melody in bars 17–18 is:

☐ a D minor chord   ☐ an E minor chord

☐ a D major chord   ☐ an E major chord.

4 The chord on the 3rd crotchet beat in bar 13 is:

☐ a dominant 7th chord   ☐ a diminished chord

☐ a tonic chord   ☐ a subdominant chord.

5 The chord in bar 23^2 (i.e. 2nd crotchet beat of bar 23) is:

☐ a supertonic chord in root position

☐ a supertonic chord in first inversion

☐ a submediant chord in root position

☐ a submediant chord in first inversion.

 ## Get the Grade

In an inverted cadence, one or both of the chords is in inversion.
- Remember the diminished chord in bar 9^3: the chord is D#, F#, A and C, with the A in the bass part. This is in the 3rd inversion – a 4/3 position chord.

Exam-style question

  The following question is a typical example of an exam question set on the prepared extract by **Mozart**. The bar numbers here refer to the extract, not where they may be found in the full score. Listen to the extract online from 1'06" to the end. **[Eduqas 12 marks]**

Menuetto da capo

(a) Identify the section of the movement that has been used in this question. **[1 mark]**

....

(b) State the key (n.b. bar numbers refer to the extract as written in the question). **[2 marks]**

   (i) At the end of the first phrase of this extract (i.e. bar 4^1) ....

   (ii) At the end of the extract (i.e. bar 12) ....

(c) Give bar and beat numbers where examples of the following musical features are found
in the score as given in the question (e.g. bar 9^3 means bar 9, crotchet beat 3). **[2 marks]**

   (i) A dominant 7th chord ....   **(ii)** A supertonic chord ....

(d) State the actual pitch of the first note played by the viola. .... **[1 mark]**

(e) Describe three features of the melody heard in this extract. **[3 marks]**

   (i) ....   **(ii)** ....   **(iii)** ....

(f) Describe three features of the rhythm heard in this extract. **[3 marks]**

   (i) ....   **(ii)** ....   **(iii)** ....

Prepared extract 2: Rainbow, 'Since You've Been Gone'

BOOK LINK: pages 196–206

Background details

- Song was originally written by Russ Ballard.

- Released in 1976.

- This version was recorded by Rainbow in 1979 and their original version can be found on their *Down to Earth* album.

Musical elements

Form and structure

The **strophic** or verse–chorus structure is shown in the following table.

Intro	Verse 1/2	Chorus 1/2	Bridge	Chorus 3	Chorus instrumental	Chorus 4
Bars 1–10	Bars 11–18 Bars 19–22 form the **pre-chorus**	Bars 23–34	Bars 35–45	Bars 46–60	Bars 61–68	Bars 69–fade

This section repeats, with different lyrics for verse 2.

Key terms

Strophic
Another name for verse–chorus form.

Pre-chorus
A short phrase immediately before the chorus.

Texture

Homophonic, generally melody + accompaniment. Some layering of patterns and motifs can be heard (e.g. end of the intro).

Instrumentation

Rock band (drums, lead and bass guitars, keyboard) and lead singer.

Tempo

Moderately bright rock beat.

Dynamics

Mostly loud (forte); bridge section is quieter (*mp* – mezzo piano moderately quiet or 'half-quiet').

Rhythm

- Time signature is 4/4 (i.e. four crotchet beats per bar).

- Lots of patterns used, complex in the melody line to follow the rhythms of the lyrics.

- Syncopation included, typical of the rock style.

Tonality

Get the Grade

4/4 time signature can also be described as **simple quadruple** time.

Intro	Verse 1/2	Chorus 1/2	Bridge	Chorus 3	Chorus instrumental	Chorus 4
G major	G major	G major	G major (includes changes of key to E minor and C major)	A major	A major	A major

- Main sections are major throughout.
- Bridge section provides more interest with a modulation to E minor and C major.
- Last three repetitions of the chorus are heard up a tone from the opening home key (i.e. A major).
- Song finishes in a different key than it started in (i.e. one tone higher).

Melody

Mostly conjunct (moves by step) with quite a wide vocal range.

Intro	Verse 1/2	Chorus 1/2	Bridge	Chorus 3	Chorus instrumental	Chorus 4
(Chords) Vocal 'oohs' – simple conjunct movement	Off-beat entry of melody 2 × 4-bar phrases, descending Word-setting is syllabic and rhythms complex to fit the words B. 19–20 (pre-chorus) – highest pitch so far	3 × 4-bar phrases Based on intro, i.e. the 'hook' vocals enter now on the strong first beats	New melody, first on lead guitar, then vocals Lower in pitch for guitar Piano improvisation with lead singer 8ve leap up in melody line at the end of each phrase	Repeat of chorus but a tone higher Vocalist – non-syllabic on 'Oh' + some melodic work in the lead guitar part Vocals have been double-tracked Includes the highest vocal pitches in the song	Lead guitar solo (improvisation)	Vocals again with 'hook' Fade-out after 6 bars

💡 **Remember**

The device of repeating the chorus a tone higher at the end of a song is common practice in pop music.

Harmony

The harmony used in this song is interesting.

- The opening four-chord pattern, G ⇒ D ⇒ Em ⇒ C, is used in three of the four sections (i.e. intro, verse and chorus), sometimes with other chords.

G	D	Em	C
(notation)	(notation)	(notation)	(notation)
G, B, D	D, F#, A	E, G, B	C, E, G

For example, this chord pattern is heard twice in the intro, each time finishing with the dominant chord of D:

- The bridge has the most varied harmonies (see table on following page).
- Root position and first inversion chords are to be found.
- Some 7th chords and suspended chords are to be found.
- Note the chords used in the second inversion (i.e. 6/4), and the one dominant 7th chord that is in second inversion (i.e. 4/3).

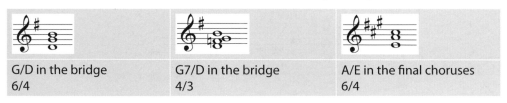

G/D in the bridge 6/4	G7/D in the bridge 4/3	A/E in the final choruses 6/4

Remember

- A root position chord means that the chords have the root note played in the bass (e.g. G, B, D with G in the bass).

- First inversion chords are chords with the third of the chord in the bass (e.g. G, B, D with B in the bass).

- A 7th chord is a triad, with the note that forms the interval of a 7th above the root. For example, G7 = G, B, D and F (instead of D, F#, A and C).

Revision tip

A chord pattern can also be known as a chord progression or a chord sequence.

Get the Grade

Learning about the chords and the harmony can be tricky to understand – but will serve you well in the examination.

Revision tips

A capital letter, e.g. G, C, F, etc., signifies a major chord built on that note.

A lower-case letter 'm' after the chord name signifies a minor chord built on that note.

- Chord changes are often two in every bar (note also the syncopated rhythms).

- Chord changes slow down to start the pre-chorus (one per bar), but quicken and are syncopated at the end of the pre-chorus.

- Each section starts with a tonic chord and ends with a dominant chord (apart from the final choruses, which end on the tonic chord to finish the piece).

- Final choruses have been transposed up by a tone, with an extra chord added.

Intro	Verses and pre-chorus	Chorus	Bridge	Final choruses
G ⇒ D ⇒ Em ⇒ C (× 2) ⇒ D	Verses:	G ⇒ D ⇒ Em ⇒ C (× 2) + D	G ⇒ Am7 ⇒ G/B* ⇒ C	A ⇒ E ⇒ F#m ⇒ D
G ⇒ D ⇒ Em ⇒ C (× 2) ⇒ D (held)	G ⇒ D/F#* ⇒ Em ⇒ D	Played three times	G/D** ⇒ B ⇒ Em ⇒ G7/D**	(× 2) ⇒ E
(Ends imperfect cadence)	C ⇒ G/B* ⇒ A ⇒ D (× 2)		C ⇒ Am7 ⇒ D7sus†	A ⇒ E ⇒ F#m ⇒ D
	Pre-chorus:		Then repeats, but note the subtle changes:	(× 2) ⇒ E
	E♭ ⇒ F		G ⇒ Am7 ⇒ G/B* ⇒ C	A ⇒ E ⇒ F#m ⇒ F
	E♭ ⇒ F/A* ⇒ Cm7 ⇒ D		G/D** ⇒ B/D#* ⇒ Em ⇒ G7/D**	A/E** ⇒ E ⇒ F#m ⇒ F
			C ⇒ Am7 ⇒ D5††	A/E** ⇒ E ⇒ A
				(Ends perfect cadence)

Revision tips

Some of the chords in the table above have been picked out as being of interest:

* These are 1st inversion chords, i.e. the 3rd of the chord is in the bass.

** These are 2nd inversion chords, i.e. the 5th of the chord is in the bass.

† This is known as a D7sus4 chord, where the 3rd of the chord (i.e. the F#) is replaced by the 4th above the root (i.e. the G). This has been suspended over from the previous chord (i.e. instead of D, F#, A, C, the suspended chord is D, **G**, A, C).

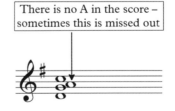

There is no A in the score – sometimes this is missed out

†† This is a D5 chord, sometimes called a 'power chord'. It consists of only two notes: the root and the 5th of the chord (i.e. the 3rd of the chord is missing). The two notes in a D5 chord are D and A.

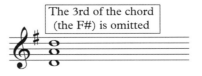

The 3rd of the chord (the F#) is omitted

Activity 2.2

1 Try answering these questions about 'Since You've Been Gone'. They are worth 1 mark each.

	True or False?
This song is in a minor key.	
This song is in a major key.	
This song is in a rock style.	
This song is in a reggae style.	
This song is performed as a cappella.	
This song is accompanied by a rock group.	
This song is accompanied by a string quartet.	

2 The cadence heard in bar 22 (end of pre-chorus) is:

(a) a plagal cadence

(b) an imperfect cadence

(c) a perfect cadence.

3 The notes of the chord D7sus4 are:

(a) D F A C

(b) D F# A C

(c) D G A C

(d) D G# A C

4 There are two intervals in the chorus melody (heard on the words 'been gone' in the first two phrases). These are:

(a) a tone then a semitone

(b) a tone then a 3rd

(c) a semitone then a tone

(d) a semitone then a 3rd.

5 Match the statements in these two columns.

The only power chord used in this piece	uses a descending minim pattern.
A chord written as D/F# means that	in the verse section of this song.
There is a modulation to D major	the second note is the one heard in the bass.
The first part of the bass line in the verse	includes a solo for the lead guitarist.
The first part of the bridge section	a syncopated chordal idea.
This piece begins with	is the chord of D5.

Exam-style questions

 The following question is a typical example of an exam question set on the prepared extract **'Since You've Been Gone'**. Listen to the extract online from 1'54" to 2'16". **[Eduqas 12 marks]**

Lyrics:

> *If you will come back*
> *Baby, you know you'll never do wrong*

(a) Identify the section heard in this extract. **[1 mark]**

....

(b) State three ways in which the opening music in this section contrasts with the previous section. **[3 marks]**

   (i) ....

   (ii) ....

   (iii) ....

(c) Name two rhythmic features used in the melody for the words *'If you will come back Baby, you know ...'* **[2 marks]**

   (i) ....

   (ii) ....

(d) Name the following: **[2 marks]**

   (i) The key at the point when the vocal line sings the word 'wrong'.

   ....

   (ii) The interval used in the vocal line on the word 'wrong'.

   ....

(e) Name the last chord heard in this extract and identify what type of chord it is. **[2 marks]**

....

(f) Underline the name of the person who wrote this song. **[1 mark]**

   Roger Glover   **Ritchie Blackmore**   **Russ Ballard**   **Ronnie Romero**

(g) Underline the date when this song was released by Rainbow. **[1 mark]**

   1976   **1977**   **1978**   **1979**

CHAPTER 3: PREPARED EXTRACTS WJEC

What Do I Need To Know?

There are two prepared extracts of music that you must learn in more detail. Each is linked to a different area of study:

▶ Rondeau, from the *Abdelazer Suite II* by Purcell

▶ 'Handbags and Gladrags' by the Stereophonics

In the Appraising examination, the Purcell question will always be question 1. The Stereophonics question will always be question 7. Both will be marked out of 9 marks (the same as all the other questions on the paper).

BOOK LINK:
pages 54–61

BOOK LINK:
pages 207–217

Prepared extract 1: Purcell, Rondeau

Background details

* The composer was Henry Purcell (1659–1695).

* From the Baroque era, generally considered to be one of the first great English composers.

* Wrote incidental music for a play called '**Abdelazer**' in 1695. The music was in nine movements, of which the **Rondeau** was the second.

* A rondeau was a structure based around a fixed pattern of repetition (influenced by a similar idea in early French poetry).

* The most common rondeau structure in music is:

Section A – repeated
Section B – repeated
Section A – not repeated
Section C – repeated
Section A – not repeated

⭐ **Revision tip**

During the later Classical period, the rondeau was expanded to become the musical form known as **rondo**.

Musical elements

Form and structure

A rondeau, in Purcell's time, had a recurring main section (or theme), which alternated with subsidiary sections (or themes).

* The overall plan of the movement is A B A C A.

* It has five distinct sections. Each section is eight bars long.

* Any repeat of the sections is often left to the discretion of the conductor. Sometimes the first section is repeated in performance; sometimes the first and the last sections are repeated in performance.

Section A	Section B	Section A	Section C	Section A
Bars 1–8	Bars 9–16	Bars 17–24	Bars 25–32	Bars 33–40
Main themes introduced – 8 bars long	Contrasting episode 1 – this uses ideas from section A but is in a different key, that of the relative major	Exact repetition of b. 1–8	Contrasting episode 2 – this uses new thematic material, again in a different key, this time starting in the dominant minor and ending in the home key	Exact repetition of b. 1–8

Texture

Homophonic: melody and accompaniment. Throughout, the melody is played by violin 1.

Instrumentation

String chamber ensemble: the score for study has four parts, just like a string quartet: violin 1, violin 2, viola and cello.

Tempo

- Not indicated on all scores; some recordings are faster than others.
- Generally, the tempo is **allegro moderato**, and has been described as having the feeling of a 'spirited hornpipe dance'.

Dynamics

- Not generally indicated on scores of the time. There is a very narrow range – often the same throughout.

Rhythm

- Triple time.
- Written as 3/2 (i.e. three minim beats in every bar).
- Simple rhythms used, some dotted rhythms.

Tonality

Section A	Section B	Section A	Section C	Section A
Bars 1–8	Bars 9–16	Bars 17–24	Bars 25–32	Bars 33–40
D minor – the home key	**F major** – the relative major. It is the mediant major	**D minor** – the home key	Starts in **A minor** – the dominant minor. Ends back in the home key **D minor** (by b. 30)	**D minor** – the home key

 Get the Grade

IMPORTANT! In exam questions, the beats may be referred to as six crotchet beats per bar. This is because it is easier to pinpoint exact chords or features in that way. For example, the beats in bar 6 may be referred to as 6^1, 6^2, 6^3, 6^4, 6^5 and 6^6.

In all instances, the questions on chords will be explained clearly in the examination question for you.

Melody

The melody in this piece contains a number of musical motifs that are used throughout the movement.

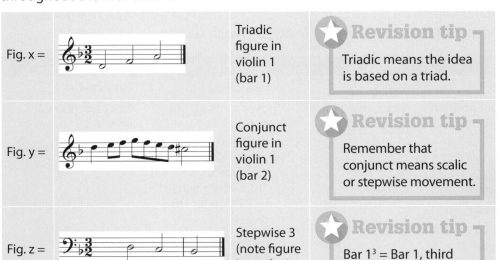

Fig. x =		Triadic figure in violin 1 (bar 1)	⭐ **Revision tip** — Triadic means the idea is based on a triad.
Fig. y =		Conjunct figure in violin 1 (bar 2)	⭐ **Revision tip** — Remember that conjunct means scalic or stepwise movement.
Fig. z =		Stepwise 3 (note figure bars 1³–2)	⭐ **Revision tip** — Bar 1³ = Bar 1, third crotchet beat.

Section A	Section B	Section A	Section C	Section A
Bars 1–8	Bars 9–16	Bars 17–24	Bars 25–32	Bars 33–40
Introduces Fig. x, Fig. y and Fig. z	Based on Fig. x and Fig. y (b. 1 and 2 of section A have been transposed at the start, up a 3rd into the key of F major)	Exact repetition of section A	New thematic material with dotted rhythm; still has the same 'feel' – derived from Fig. y	Exact repetition of section A
Fig. x = triadic idea, ascending	Fig. 'z' developed from b. 11 onwards			
Fig. y = stepwise, conjunct idea	Use of certain intervals: Perfect 4ths (b. 9⁵–10, 10⁵–11) Octaves (b. 11⁵⁻⁶ and 12⁵⁻⁶) a perfect 5th (b. 15⁶–16)		One interval of a 5th (b. 28⁵ –29¹). All other movement is stepwise (conjunct)	
Fig. z = stepwise descending 3 note fig. (b. 1³–2¹, cello)			B. 28: Fig. z, now in violin 1 and incorporating the dotted rhythm B. 29: melodic sequence B. 32: new cadential idea	

- The pitch range in each part is quite narrow.
- Melodic ideas include both conjunct and disjunct movement.

Harmony

The harmony is described as diatonic. In the Appraising examination, you could be asked to describe or identify any chord or key at any point – such details are to be found in the textbook. For revision purposes, this guide identifies the main harmonic features in each section.

BOOK LINK: pages 54–61

Section A	Section B	Section A	Section C	Section A
Bars 1–8	Bars 9–16	Bars 17–24	Bars 25–32	Bars 33–40
Mainly root position and 1st inversion chords	Mainly root position and 1st inversion chords	Exact repetition of section A	Uses a mix of root position and 1st inversion chords: there is one 2nd inversion (b. 28^1); one 3rd inversion chord (b. 32^2); some 7th chords	Exact repetition of section A
			Begins in A minor. End of b. 28 (1st 4-bar phrase) – perfect cadence in A major (#3 in viola)	
End of b. 2: imperfect cadence (iv–V in D minor)	End of b. 10: imperfect cadence (IV–V in F major)		B. 29: the continuing A major chord now acts as V of the home key	
Cycle of 5ths (b. 2^5– 6^5)	Use of 7th chords is again evident, including 7ths (e.g. 13$^{5-6}$)		B. 30: D minor	
			B. 31: opening chord is a diminished chord on C# (**the only one in the movement**)	
Some secondary 7th chords in first inversion (e.g. b. 7^1)	Some chords are in 2nd inversion (end of b. 11; b. 15^3; b. 16 – 2nd chord)		Ends with imperfect cadence (known as a **Phrygian cadence**), i.e. iv6^3 ⟹ V	
B. 8: dominant 7th chord (A7) Perfect cadence in D minor to finish section A	Perfect cadence in F major to finish section B – note V7 (dominant 7th/C7) on b. 16^3			

 Remember

Phrygian cadence

A particular type of imperfect cadence, iv6^3 ⟹ V, with the semitone step down in the bass from B♭ to A.

Activity 3.1

Have a go at answering these multiple-choice questions on harmony. They are worth 1 mark each.

1 The chord at the start of bar 3 is:

☐ major in root position

☐ minor in 1st inversion

☐ major in 1st inversion

☐ minor in root position

2 The chord in bar 10, minim beat 3 (i.e. the 5th crotchet beat) is:

☐ a tonic in root position

☐ a subdominant in 1st inversion

☐ a tonic in 2nd inversion

☐ a dominant in root position

3 The chord that supports the melody in all of bar 29 is:

☐ an A minor chord

☐ an A major chord

☐ an E minor chord

☐ an E major chord

4 The chord on the 2nd crotchet beat in bar 32 is a tonic 4/2 chord. Is this:

☐ the tonic minor 7th in root position?

☐ the tonic minor 7th in 1st inversion?

☐ the tonic minor 7th in 2nd inversion?

☐ the tonic minor 7th in 3rd inversion?

5 The chord in bar 37³ (i.e. 3rd crotchet beat of bar 37) is:

☐ a subdominant chord in root position

☐ a subdominant chord in 1st inversion

☐ a submediant chord in root position

☐ a submediant chord in 1st inversion

Exam-style question

 The following question is a typical example of an exam question set on the prepared extract by Purcell. Listen to the score below online from 36" to the end then answer the following questions.

[WJEC 9 marks]

(a) Identify the section of the Rondeau that has been used in this question. **[1 mark]**

....

(b) State the key: **[2 marks]**

  (i) at the start of this extract ....

  (ii) at the end of this extract ....

(c) Give bar and beat numbers where examples of the following musical features are found in the score (e.g. bar 9^6 means bar 9, crotchet beat 6) **[2 marks]**

Features	Bars
A dominant 7th chord	
A diminished chord	

(d) State the actual pitch of the last note played by the viola .... **[1 mark]**

(e) Describe three features of the melody heard in this extract. **[3 marks]**

  (i) .... **(ii)** .... **(iii)** ....

Prepared extract 2: Stereophonics, 'Handbags and Gladrags'

Background

BOOK LINK:
pages 207–217

- Song was written in 1967 by Mike D'Abo.
- Previously recorded by Chris Farlowe (1967) and also Rod Stewart (1969).
- Re-released by the Stereophonics in 2001.

Musical elements

Form and structure

- **Strophic** verse structure, with **refrain**.
- Includes a number of instrumental interludes based on the introduction.

 Key terms

Strophic
Another name for verse–chorus form.

Refrain
A repeated line within the verse.

Intro	Verses 1, 2 + refrain + instrumental interlude	Verse 3 + refrain + instrumental interlude	Verse 3 (repeat + shortened) + refrain	Outro
Bars 1–6	Bars 7–24/26	Bars 27–44	Bars 35–40	Bars 45–53
Instrumental	Verses 1 + 2 (b. 7–18) Refrain (b. 19–20) Instrumental (bars 21–24 same as intro) (b. 25–26) + 2nd time bar, with extension	Verse 3 (b. 27–38) Refrain × 3 (b. 39–44) • 1st vocal • 2nd/3rd instrumental interlude	Verse 3 (shorter: b. 35–38 – last 4 bars only) Refrain (b. 39–40)	Instrumental (b. 45–53) As intro but 3 bars added

← This section is repeated, with different lyrics for verse 2 →

Texture

- Homophonic, generally melody + accompaniment.
- Lighter texture at the opening, although other musical ideas are layered to add interest in the verses.
- Piano riff and acoustic guitar only to finish.

Instrumentation

- Rock group (drum kit, bass guitar, acoustic/electric guitar) with added orchestral instruments (strings, brass and oboe); piano/organ.
- Drum kit: played with brushes for intro + verse, louder with sticks for 2nd part of verse + refrain.
- Male singer (high) – gentle vocal tone in verse (although 'raspy') – more of a 'rock' quality in refrain.
- The accompaniment is very simple at times (e.g. minim chords, as in the opening – an idea that repeats in bar 27), although at other times it has more pace and interest to fit in with the rock ballad style.

Tempo

- ♩ = 64 (a metronome marking, which means the tempo has been measured in beats per minute), which is quite a slow beat.

- Feels as if the pace quickens in refrain as the bass line has more movement.

Dynamics

- Piano/quiet in verse, forte and louder in refrain.

Rhythm

- Time signature is 4/4 (i.e. four crotchet beats per bar).

- Begins simply, but soon extends to include a range of rhythms with some quite tricky patterns (particularly in the vocal line to accommodate the words), with semiquavers, dotted notes, syncopation and one bar of 9/8 time (bar 26), which is known as triple compound time.

Tonality

Every section of this song begins in the key of B♭ major, and includes a modulation to E♭ major. The song finishes in B♭ major.

Melody

Intro	Verses 1, 2 + refrain + instrumental interlude	Verse 3 + refrain + instrumental interlude	Verse 3 (repeat + shortened) + refrain	Outro
Bars 1–6	:Bars 7–24/26	Bars 27–44 :	Bars 35–40	Bars 45–53
Opens with 5-bar melody Finishes with piano 'riff' Lots of disjunct movement; intervals used: 4ths + 5ths	Word-setting here is syllabic Short phrases Range is a 9th All 4 lines are similar in styling Mix of conjunct and disjunct movement Tricky rhythms, to fit the lyrics	Changes in the melody: • for variety • to accommo-date lyrics Vocal part reaches highest notes in this section (Vocal idea on 'Oh' is non-syllabic) New melodic idea in instrumental – syncopated riff + extended idea (organ)	Only a part of verse is repeated. Changes here are: • quieter dynamic • lighter style accompaniment	Opening of oboe motif reinforced by other instruments Closing phrases use the opening piano riff

Harmony

The harmony used in this song is repetitive. Apart from the two chords of E♭ ⇒ F9sus4 used in the refrain, it is based on two chord patterns. Each uses four chords.

✔ Get the Grade

4/4 time signature can also be described as **simple quadruple** time.

⭐ Revision tip

To find the modulation to E♭ major in each section, look out for the A♭ in the music, or in the guitar chord symbols.

⭐ Revision tip

Remember that the word-setting for most of this song is **syllabic**, i.e. one note per syllable.

Chord pattern 1: B♭ ⇒ B♭/A♭ ⇒ E♭/G ⇒ F9sus4

B♭	B♭ / A♭	E♭ / G	F9sus4
B♭	B♭/A♭	E♭/G	F9(sus4)
B♭, D, F	A♭, B♭, D, F	G, B♭, E♭	F, G, B♭, E♭

Revision tip

F9sus4 is the way the chord is labelled on the sheet music. Another way of thinking about it is as chord IV (i.e. E flat, G and B flat) with the dominant note in the bass (i.e. F).

Chord pattern 2: Gm ⇒ F ⇒ B♭ ⇒ C

Gm	F	B♭	C
Gm	F	B♭	C
G, B♭, D	F, A, C	B♭, D, F	C, E, G

Revision tip

A chord pattern can also be known as a 'chord progression' or a 'chord sequence'.

Intro	Verses 1, 2 + refrain + instrumental interlude	Verse 3 + refrain + instrumental interlude	Verse 3 (repeat + shortened) + refrain	Outro
Bars 1–6	:Bars 7–24/26	Bars 27–44 :	Bars 35–40	Bars 45–53
Chord pattern 1: 2 chords per bar	Verse: Chord pattern 1 × 4	Verse: Chord pattern 1 × 4 (but F7 not F9sus4 in first 2 repetitions)	Verse: (Shortened – NO chord pattern 1 here)	Instrumental : Chord pattern 1 × 4
Played 3 times (i.e. × 3)				B♭ major chord to end
Stepwise movement in bass supports the harmony	Bars 15–18 Chord pattern 2 × 1: 1 chord per bar Refrain: based on 2 chords – E♭ ⇒ F9sus4 Instrumental: Chord pattern 1 × 2 2nd time bar: B♭–F9sus4 added Ends imperfect cadence	Chord pattern 2 × 1 Refrain: based on 2 chords – E♭ ⇒ F9sus4 Instrumental: Chord pattern 1 × 2 Ends imperfect cadence	Chord pattern 2 × 1 Refrain: based on 2 chords – E♭ ⇒ F9sus4 Ends imperfect cadence	Ends perfect cadence
Ends imperfect cadence (E♭– F9sus4)				

 Get the Grade

The G minor chord is the only minor chord used in this song, so it is worth remembering where it is.
- It is heard in bar 15 – just before the lyric 'So what becomes of you my love' – the phrase before the first refrain.
- Also heard in bar 35 – just before the lyric 'They told me you missed school today' – start of (shortened) verse 3.

Activity 3.2

Complete the following quiz on 'Handbags and Gladrags'. Each question is worth 1 mark.

1

	True or False?
This song is in a minor key.	
This song is in a major key.	
This song is in a reggae style.	
This song is in a rock ballad style.	
This song is performed as a cappella.	
This song is accompanied by a woodwind quartet.	
This song is accompanied by a rock group with additional instruments.	

2 The cadence heard at bars 48^4–49^1 (outro, end of the 4th bar–5th bar) is:

(a) a plagal cadence

(b) an imperfect cadence

(c) a perfect cadence

3 The notes of the chord F9sus4 are:

(a) F A C E♭

(b) F A B♭ E♭

(c) F G B♭ E♭

4 The first two intervals of the opening melody in the introduction are:

(a) a 5th followed by a 3rd

(b) a 5th followed by a 4th

(c) a 5th followed by a 5th

(d) a 5th followed by a 6th

5 Match the beginning of the statement in the first column with what completes it in the right column.

The only minor chord used in this piece	uses a dotted rhythm pattern.
A chord written as B♭/A♭ means that	includes an upwards suspension.
One bar in this song	the second note is the one heard in the bass.
The first part of the bass line in the outro	is the chord of G minor.
The last bar of the piece	a descending minim idea in the bass.
This piece begins with	has a different time signature than the rest.

 Revision tip

Bar 48^4 means: the 4th (and last) beat of bar 48.

Bar 49^1 means: the 1st beat of bar 49.

Exam-style question

The following question is a typical example of an exam question set on the prepared extract **'Handbags and Gladrags'**.

Listen to the extract online from 3'38" to the end of the song.　　　　**[WJEC 9 marks]**

The **lyrics** in this section are:

> *They told me you missed school today,*
> *So what I suggest you just throw them all away.*
> *The handbags and the gladrags*
> *That your poor old granddad had to sweat to buy you.*
> (Instrumental to close)

(a) This extract consists of two sections. Identify the two sections.　　　　**[2 marks]**

....

....

(b) (i) Name the first chord in this extract, heard at the beginning of the section.　　　　**[1 mark]**

....

(ii) Name the last chord heard in this extract.　　　　**[1 mark]**

....

(c) Describe three features of the instrumental accompaniment in this extract.　　　　**[3 marks]**

 (i) ....

 (ii) ....

(iii) ....

(d) The melody heard **after** the singer has finished singing the words '*... had to sweat to buy you*' has been used a number of times before in the song. Underline the section where it was first heard.　　　　**[1 mark]**

　　　　Introduction　　　　Verse 1　　　　Refrain　　　　Verse 2

(e) Underline the date when this song was originally composed.　　　　**[1 mark]**

　　　　1957　　　　1967　　　　1977　　　　1987

CHAPTER 4: AURAL DICTATION

What Do I Need To Know?

▶ One of the questions in the Appraising paper will be presented along with an outline score of the melody heard in the extract.

▶ In this question, you will be asked to complete the rhythm or pitch of a short section of the music.

▶ Pitch dictation will always be within the major scale.

▶ Pitch dictation could be in the treble or bass clef.

▶ Rhythm and pitch dictation will always be in simple time.

▶ Recognition of musical patterns could be in simple or compound time.

▶ Other parts of the question will require you to identify other musical features (e.g. keys, cadences, time signatures, recognition of instruments/voices, any signs or terms used in the given outline score).

💡 Remember

- Simple time – 2/4, 3/4, 4/4
- Compound time – 6/8

Many GCSE Music students find musical dictation a challenging skill – so the quicker you embrace this and do everything you can to improve your reading and writing skills in music, the better.

This question could be found in any area of study, and will be based on an unprepared musical extract. You will be given an outline score as part of the question – and you will be required, at some point, to 'fill in the gaps' as it were.

Confidence in being able to answer this question will come from knowing and recognising:

- key signatures
- time signatures
- stepwise (conjunct) movement
- intervals (disjunct/angular) movement
- patterns in pitch and rhythm.

☑ Get the Grade

Make sure you know:
- the time signatures (2/4, 3/4, 4/4 and 6/8)
- all the different types of note-values
- key signatures up to four flats and four sharps (major and minor).

Don't avoid musical notation just because it seems complicated. Music is a language, and the more you use notation the better and more fluent you will be at reading and writing it. You need to complete lots of theoretical exercises and learn to sight-read; take it slowly, one step at a time.

Relating the sound to the symbol is what is important.

Some suggested activities are given in the final section of the *WJEC/Eduqas GCSE Music* textbook.

The best method is to build your memory skills slowly but steadily. As a young child, you learned how to speak and write by copying and repeating phrases

BOOK LINK:
pages 248–253

before writing them down – and in learning musical language, you must do the same. Copy and repeat musical fragments, then try writing them down.

Listen to lots of short three- or four-note melodic and rhythmic patterns. Copy and repeat the pattern, then visualise how the idea would look if written down. Gradually, you will be able to copy and work out more complex patterns in different keys.

Test yourself: how accurately can you copy and write what you play and hear?

Activity 4.1

You can improve your skills without listening to any music. Think of an easy melody and see if you can write the tune down. Then go to a keyboard or instrument of your choice and play what you have written. If it doesn't sound anything like you expected it to, then persevere and work out why. For example, you could try 'Away in a Manger' in the key of C major. This is in 3/4 time and the first note is a G. Work out the pitches, then the rhythm.

Now try writing it in the key of A major and again in E major.

Activity 4.2

Look at some pieces of music (ideally, short notated melodies). Tap out the rhythms. Give yourself the pitch of the first note, then try to sight-sing and play the melodies. This will really help to improve your music reading skills.

Activity 4.3

Compose some two-bar musical phrases in a variety of different keys and time signatures. You can keep a note of them however you wish – notate them on manuscript paper or using technology. Perform or play them to a friend to see if they can work out what the patterns and motifs are. You could give the starting note and ending note if you wish.

Activity 4.4

The following exercises will focus on:

- identification of pitch and rhythms
- time signatures
- pitch and rhythmic dictation
- keys
- chords and cadences.

1 Listen to the following extracts online, then for each one identify:

- the correct melodic pattern heard in bars 3 and 4
- the time signature
- the key.

(a)

Identify the melodic pattern heard in bars 3 and 4 by ticking the correct answer from the three choices below:

1	**2**	**3**
☐	☐	☐

State the time signature:

State the key:

(b)

Identify the melodic pattern heard in bars 3 and 4 by ticking the correct answer from the three choices below:

1	**2**	**3**
☐	☐	☐

State the time signature:

State the key:

(c)

Identify the melodic pattern heard in bars 3 and 4 by ticking the correct answer from the three choices below:

1	**2**	**3**
☐	☐	☐

State the time signature:

State the key:

(d)

Identify the melodic pattern heard in bars 3 and 4 by ticking the correct answer from the three choices below:

1	**2**	**3**
☐	☐	☐

State the time signature:

State the key:

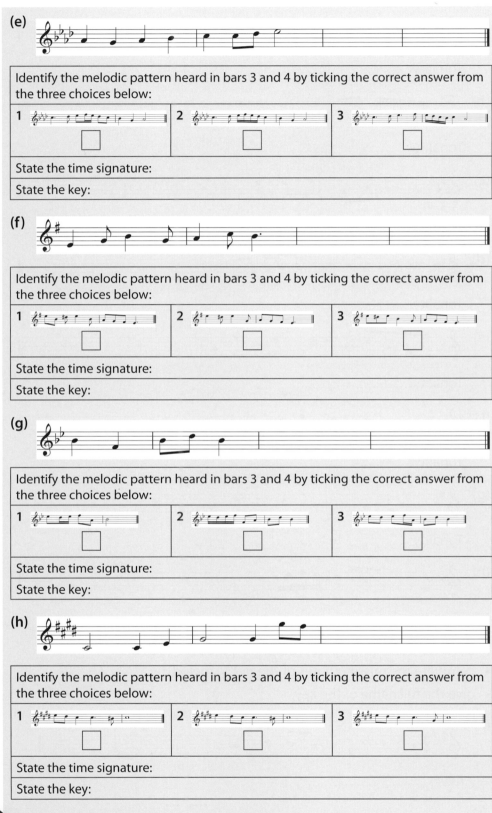

(e)

Identify the melodic pattern heard in bars 3 and 4 by ticking the correct answer from the three choices below:

State the time signature:

State the key:

(f)

Identify the melodic pattern heard in bars 3 and 4 by ticking the correct answer from the three choices below:

State the time signature:

State the key:

(g)

Identify the melodic pattern heard in bars 3 and 4 by ticking the correct answer from the three choices below:

State the time signature:

State the key:

(h)

Identify the melodic pattern heard in bars 3 and 4 by ticking the correct answer from the three choices below:

State the time signature:

State the key:

2 Listen to the following extracts online, then for each one:

- insert the correct time signature
- insert the missing **rhythm** in bars 3 and 4
- state whether you think the tonality may be **major** or **minor**.

(a)

Tonality: ....

(b)

Tonality: ....

(c)

Tonality: ....

(d)

Tonality: ....

(e)

Tonality: ....

Get the Grade

If you have managed to notate the rhythm of these examples – why not try to work out the pitch as well? Every extra task will help to improve your skill.

(f)

Tonality: ....

(g)

Tonality: ....

(h)

Tonality: ....

3 Listen to the following extracts online, then for each one:

* complete the missing notes of the treble melody

* give the full name of the key.

(a)

Key: ....

(b)

Key: ....

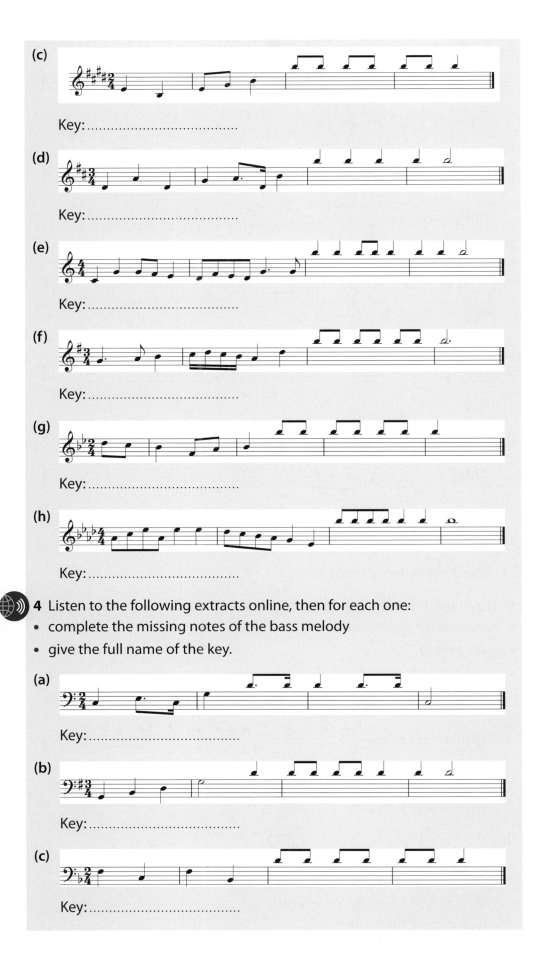

(c) Key:.................................

(d) Key:.................................

(e) Key:.................................

(f) Key:.................................

(g) Key:.................................

(h) Key:.................................

4 Listen to the following extracts online, then for each one:
- complete the missing notes of the bass melody
- give the full name of the key.

(a) Key:.................................

(b) Key:.................................

(c) Key:.................................

Get the Grade

Challenge yourself. As you listen to these examples, can you identify what type of chord is marked by the star in some of them?

(d)

Key: ....

(e)

Key: ....

(f)

Key: ....

(g)

Key: ....

(h)

Cadence?   Cadence?

Key: ....

Name the cadence in bar 2: ....

Name the cadence in bar 4: ....

 5 Listen to the following extracts online, then for each one:

- complete the missing notes of the melody
- state the key
- name the type of time signature (i.e. simple duple, simple triple, simple quadruple or compound duple).

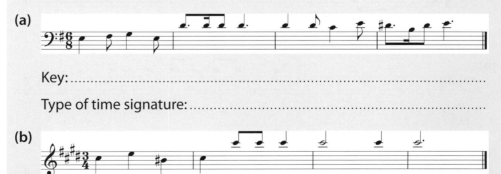

(a)

Key: ....

Type of time signature: ....

(b)

Key: ....

Type of time signature: ....

(c)

Key: ....

Type of time signature: ....

(d)

Key: ....

Type of time signature: ....

(e)

Key: ....

Type of time signature: ....

(f)

Key: ....

Type of time signature: ....

(g)

Key: ....

Type of time signature: ....

(h)

Key: ....

Type of time signature: ....

(i)

Key: ....

Type of time signature: ....

(j)

Key: ....

Type of time signature: ....

6 Listen to the following extracts online, then for each one:
- name the **cadence** heard at the end of the musical phrase
- state whether the tonality is **Major** or **Minor**.

	Cadence?	Major or Minor?
(i)		
(ii)		
(iii)		
(iv)		
(v)		
(vi)		
(vii)		
(viii)		
(ix)		
(x)		

CHAPTER 5: EXAM-STYLE QUESTIONS

What Do I Need To Know?

For some of the questions in the Appraising paper, you need to write longer, more extended answers in response to the musical extracts that are played in the examination.

You will have to show that you can make accurate musical observations and, where appropriate, your answers must show understanding of:

The musical elements such as: • dynamics • harmony • instruments/voice • melody • rhythm/metre • structure • tempo • texture • timbre • tonality	**The musical contexts** such as: • the effect of the occasion/ venue • the purpose and intention of the music • the social, historical and cultural background	**The musical language** such as: • treble notation • bass notation • viola clef (prepared extracts on AoS 1) • chord symbols • key signatures • musical vocabulary • rhythm notation • time signatures

In both the WJEC and Eduqas examinations, there are basically two types of questions.

1 Short answer questions: your answer needs to be precise, as you may be asked to name, state, identify, underline, give, pick, insert or define something. This often includes a type of multiple-choice question, where you have to select the correct answer.

2 Longer answer questions: you may be asked to describe, explain, compare, contrast, complete the missing pitch or rhythm, or point out the musical differences between the extracts of music played in the examination.

You will see examples of the short answer questions elsewhere in this book, so in this chapter we will look at the longer answer questions. There are two types.

1 The first requires an answer which will be a long paragraph

2 The second will be more of an essay-style answer. For many students, this can be more challenging.

⭐ Revision tip

Most of the questions in the examination are to do with the elements of music and the language of music. This is why it is so important that you know exactly what to include in your answers.

Writing a long paragraph-style answer

These questions may be worth anything from 2 to 6 marks, with 1 mark awarded for each correct comment or observation. No room for irrelevant details here! Let us look at an example.

Example of a long paragraph-style answer

 Listen online to the first 58 seconds of some jazz music. In the examination, the extract will be played twice. Two different questions are presented below, which are typical examples of what may be asked on this extract.

Question 1 Explain three ways in which the composer creates a relaxed type of mood in the music.   **[3 marks]**

High mark answer	Commentary
The composer has used a slow tempo, with a steady moving, regular beat. The dynamic of the music is generally 'piano', and the regular and steady slow-type melody played by the bass in a low register adds to the feel. There is also a gentle percussive beat on the drums, and the use of brushes makes the effect softer, which is quite calming.	*This is a very good answer showing clearly that the student has considered a range of musical elements, including explanation of the way that the instruments have been used.*
Lower mark answer	*Commentary*
The way the piano plays supports the mood. The drums are played softly, which helps the beat. The feeling is chilled-out and relaxed.	*Some observations are correct but there is a lack of explanation. The student needs to **describe** the way the piano plays to create the mood, i.e. how and what is playing, and what type of drum beat is used. The final sentence only repeats the information already given in the question.*

Question 2 Describe how the composer uses the musical elements of **rhythm** and **metre** in this composition.   **[4 marks]**

High mark answer	Commentary
The composer has used a slow tempo (possibly lento), with a steady, moving, regular beat. This is supported by the bass line which mostly supports with crotchet beats, though moves to quavers and some off-beat patterns when it takes on the melody. There are chords in the piano part, which are mostly syncopated. The piece is in 4/4 time (i.e. simple quadruple).	*This is an excellent answer which offers plenty of accurate information using appropriate technical vocabulary. Lots of specific, relevant detail has been included.*
Lower mark answer	*Commentary*
The drums are playing a slow beat. The music is off-beat in a jazzy style, and the metre has a time signature with the same amount of beats in every bar. The composer has used the elements of rhythm and metre in an interesting way.	*The answer has included some accurate rhythmic features, but it clearly lacks the detail and explanation of the previous answer. For example, what is the time signature in the music – exactly how many beats are there in every bar? What could the tempo marking be?* *Once again, the last sentence has repeated the question, without giving exact musical details to explain **why** it may be interesting.* *If each point had been explained, higher marks would be awarded.*

Writing an essay-style answer

The essay-style answer question is worth more marks. Your answer does not need to be an 'essay' and can be presented by using bullet points, for example, but you must be sure to explain and describe your observations, not just present bullet point answers.

It is marked out of 9 in the WJEC specification, out of 10 in Eduqas, and is assessed using a marking grid that is divided into bands based on different criteria according to the question set.

Following is an example of the criteria for marking an answer that required the candidate to comment on the use of musical elements in a piece. You need to aim for the top!

A **perceptive** answer, giving a detailed description of the use of musical elements. Well organised, using appropriate terminology, with accurate grammar, punctuation and spelling.

A **secure** answer, giving a reasonable description of the use of musical elements. Mostly organised, using appropriate terminology, with generally accurate grammar, punctuation and spelling.

An **inconsistent** answer, with some description of the use of musical elements. Partly organised, with some appropriate terminology, and reasonably accurate grammar, punctuation and spelling.

A **basic** answer, with little description of the use of musical elements. Basic level of organisation and use of terminology, with errors in grammar, punctuation and spelling.

A **limited** answer, with very little description of the use of musical elements. Organisation and use of terminology is also limited, with many errors in grammar, punctuation and spelling.

Note: A mark of 0 will be given if none of the information is relevant or accurate, or if the answer has not been attempted.

Example of an essay-style question

 Listen online from the start to 1'02" from a piece of musical theatre called **'You Are the Light of the World'** from *Godspell* by Stephen Schwartz. In the examination, the extract will be played three times. The lyrics have been provided, and you may find it helpful to refer to the line numbers in your answer. **[9 or 10 marks – typical of WJEC and Eduqas]**

This is a vocal piece – here are the lyrics:

1 You are the light of the world!

2 You are the light of the world!

3 But if that light is under a bushel

4 Brrr, it's lost something kind of crucial

5 You got to stay bright to be the light of the world!

6 You are the salt of the earth,

7 You are the salt of the earth

8 But if that salt has lost its flavour,

9 It ain't got much in its favour

10 You can't have that fault and be the salt of the earth!

11 So let your light so shine before men

12 Let your light so shine

13 So that they might know some kindness again

14 We all need help to feel fine ...
   (Let's have some wine!)

Question: Describe the use of musical elements in the extract. You may refer to:

- structure
- rhythm
- dynamics
- melody

- harmony
- texture
- style
- mood.

Get the Grade

There is no one set way to answer this question. It really is all about putting in as many correct musical observations as possible. Here are some suggestions:

1 Write an essay dealing with each of the suggested elements in turn, mentioning the line numbers when you want to explain something directly in reference to the music.

2 Start your answer with a general information paragraph which applies to the whole extract, then pick out musical features of particular interest by referring to the lines of the lyrics.

Tip: You can use bullet points or side-headings in your answer, but you **must** explain your observations fully.

 Revision tip

In this list of musical elements, there's no mention of the use of instrumentation, voices or tonality. You will also gain marks if you include relevant comments on these features.

Important: The question here suggests that you 'may' refer to the points listed, so they are guidelines only. If the question clearly says 'You **must** refer to ...', then there is no element of choice. You must describe everything in the list.

Let's take a look at some answers for this question.

High mark answer A	Commentary
The *structure* of the extract falls into four sections: an introduction, two verses and a bridge, or link section.	This answer includes many excellent observations. Perhaps the one thing to add would be more exact reference to the lyrics, i.e. being really specific when pin-pointing the musical features. One good example of this was the information about the musical textures, where line numbers were given as explanation.
The *rhythms* of the piece fall into 4/4 time (simple quadruple). Dotted rhythms, tied notes, accented off-beat chords and syncopated rhythmic ideas may be heard throughout the music. The *tempo* is steady (moderato), with driving rhythms.	
The *dynamics* are forte, mostly the same throughout.	
The *melody* is very 'catchy'. The opening includes a strong riff in the bass, repeated four times in all, and the main tune is quite 'bluesy' in character. The range of the melody in the verses in quite narrow, although it is extended in the bridge section.	
The *instruments* play the accompaniment and this is known as the 'pit band', which typically includes a drum kit, bass guitar, lead guitar and keyboard (including an organ).	
The *harmony* is diatonic, and includes 'jazzy' chords such as 7ths. The extract is in a major key, ending with an imperfect cadence.	
The *texture* throughout is mostly homophonic. Verse 1 is the melody sung by a male vocalist accompanied by chords, with some harmonies also added by the chorus, while verse 2 begins in harmony with a female vocalist added. The chorus joins in fully in the bridge section (line 11) and line 14 is sung unaccompanied and in unison (monophonic *texture*).	
The music is in a kind of rock *style*, but it does also have a feeling of gospel music. It is an up-beat song with a feel-good mood.	

High mark answer B	Commentary
• Structure: the extract falls into four sections: an instrumental introduction (4 bars), two verses (lines 1–5 and 6–10) and a short chorus (line 11–the end of the extract).	Another excellent and very detailed answer. It includes lots of musical details, linked clearly to the lyrics. This is typical of a student response at the highest level, and credit will be given for the appropriate detail, organisation and correct use of subject terminology.
• Tonality: major key overall.	
• Time signature: 4/4 time (simple quadruple).	
• Texture: mostly homophonic.	
• Tempo: steady (moderato) and with driving rhythms.	
• Dynamics: forte, mostly the same throughout.	
• Instrumental accompaniment: made up of 'pit band', i.e. a drum kit, bass guitar, lead guitar and keyboard (including an organ).	
• Harmony: diatonic with quite a 'jazzy' feel.	
• Style: although the music is in a kind of rock style, it also has a feeling of gospel music. It is an up-beat song with a feel-good mood.	
• OTHER DETAILS:	
Instrumental introduction: four bars long. It begins with a descending slide (glissando) in the bass which leads into a strong, syncopated bass riff pattern, heard four times. The accented chord in the lead guitars Is on the 2nd beat (off-beat).	
Verse 1 (lines 1–5): line 1 begins with the male vocalist (this is mid-range, possibly a tenor). The chorus join in unison (line 2). Lines 3 and 4 are delivered in a kind of 'spoken style' (typical of musical theatre), and unaccompanied except for ff chords on the first beat of the bar. Line 6 – all vocalists sing in harmony.	

(continued on page 62)

High mark answer B (*continued*)	Commentary
Verse 2 (lines 6–10): In line 6, a female vocalist is added in harmony to a repeat of the tune, sung by the male tenor soloist), followed by line 7 heard in the same manner as verse 1, with all singers of the ensemble in harmony. The spoken-style delivery is heard again in lines 8 and 9, though with a type of wood-block or rim-shot played on every beat this time. All singers join, as before, for the last line of verse 2 (10). This leads without break into the chorus. Chorus (line 11–end of extract): performed by full ensemble, in harmony. There are short bursts of melody (countermelodies) adding interest by the lead guitarist and organ. Line 14 is unaccompanied and in unison, with drums added at the end of the phrase leading to the last 'spoken' type phrase from the tenor soloist. This feels like an imperfect cadence, as the music does not feel 'finished'.	

Lower mark answer	Commentary
This piece starts with an introduction before the first verse, and the voice comes in. The music has steady beats in every bar and is in a major key as it sounds happy. There is a person singing the main tune, and there is a choir backing. The first idea is repeated, and sometimes there is singing without any accompaniment. The music is mostly loud and there are guitars and a drum kit. It is like a rock-style piece. The harmony is good and works very well, and the rhythm is interesting.	*There are some accurate points made here, which will be worthy of marks. A number of the elements have been covered, but the answer lacks the explanation of the model answer, and the use of specific subject terminology is more limited. For example, the last sentence gives the opinion of the candidate, but the opportunity to say **why** the harmony is 'good' or **why** the rhythm is 'interesting' has been missed. More credit will be given for describing the actual content – so try to work out what's actually going on in the music.*

✔ Get the Grade

This is an instrumental extract, so a good overall plan would be to base your observations on **Model answer A**, i.e. comment on each of the elements in turn:

- structure
- rhythm
- dynamics
- melody
- harmony
- texture
- style
- mood.

Activity 5.1

Answer the following essay-style question.

 Listen online from the start to 1'10" to an extract from a piece of film music, the opening from the soundtrack of the film ***Rocky*** by Bill Conti. In the examination, it will be played three times.

Question: This extract is taken from the opening of the film *Rocky*, which is about a small-time boxer from working-class Philadelphia, who has been chosen to take on the heavyweight champion of the world in the boxing ring. Explain how this music is appropriate as the opening theme for the film.

In your answer refer to:

- the musical elements
- the purpose and intention of the music.   **[9 or 10 marks]**

(This is a longer answer question. If you want to attempt this answer you will need to use separate sheets of paper.)

Revision tip

Remember, you can also comment on instrumentation and tonality.

The comparison question

You will hear two versions of a piece of music. There may be some short answer questions on the extracts to start, then follows the part of the question that asks you to compare the two extracts. When describing Version 1, you will need to make points about the musical elements that you can identify. When describing Version 2, you need to concentrate on the **differences** in the music.

 Get the Grade

The marks in this type of question are given as one mark for every correct observation, with the focus on stating the 'differences' between the two pieces.

Example of a comparison question

 Listen online to the two versions of *Layla*, originally performed by Derek and the Dominos. In the examination, each version will be played three times:

Version 1: 'Layla': Derek and the Dominos; listen from the start to 0'58".

Version 2: 'Layla': Eric Clapton – unplugged; listen from the start of 1'26".

Compare the two versions, referring to contrasts in **instrumentation** and any **other features of interest**. When describing Version 2, you need to concentrate on the **differences** in the music. **[6 marks]**

High mark answer		Commentary
Version 1 **Instrumentation:** Rock group set-up, with two lead guitars; male solo and backing vocals join in on the chorus with the word 'Layla' and the last line of the chorus. The guitars start the piece and drums join in half-way through the introduction after about four bars. **Other features of interest:** The piece is in a minor key and is in 4/4 time. Guitar parts are playing repeated riffs in the introduction and the chorus, with some improvised lines during the verse. Heavy rock style (forte dynamic), with guitar hammer-ons and power chords, vocal range is quite narrow and repeats the main idea.	**Differences in Version 2** **Instrumentation:** Acoustic set-up with electro-acoustic guitars, piano and percussion including tambourine. Guitar-playing style is different – including finger-picking and strumming. Vocal singing is more gentle (piano dynamic), with female backing singers this time. **Other features of interest:** In a slower tempo, and more of a ballad style. The melody notes of the riff have been changed, and guitar now improvises during the introduction. Backing singers sing more in the chorus – not just repeating the name 'Layla', but singing longer phrases in harmony.	*This is an answer which offers a lot of accurate information, well beyond what is needed to gain full marks in this question.* *The comments for Version 2 focus on the differences, which is what has been asked for.*

Low mark answer		Commentary
Version 1 **Instrumentation:** Pop group with singer. Some drum fills are heard.	**Differences in Version 2** **Instrumentation:** Not so much drumming, more played on the piano than Version 1.	*This includes some valid points but lacks specific musical details. Less information offered here.*
Other features of interest: Rock style, which is popular. A famous song written by Eric Clapton. Quite a long introduction using repetition.	**Other features of interest:** This version does not use electric instruments, and it is a sadder style.	

 Remember

There is no credit for negative responses. For example, don't write something such as, 'There are no violins in this piece.'

 Get the Grade

Go through all the musical elements for ideas on what you can include in your answer. Respond to all sections of the question, as the answer is marked 'holistically'. This means your response will be judged overall – you do not get marks awarded for every correct point.

Exam-style questions

The following exam question has been set out both in the format of the Eduqas examination (12 marks) and the WJEC examination (9 marks).

 Revision tip

While preparing for the WJEC question, listening to the extra versions in the Eduqas question will give you additional practice in preparing for this type of question (and vice versa). It's worth giving it a go.

Eduqas

 Listen online to three versions of '**The House of the Rising Sun**'. In the examination, each version will be played **twice**. **[Total 12 marks]**

Version 1: 'House of the Rising Sun'; listen from start to 0'46"

Version 2: 'House of the Rising Sun'; listen from start to 1'33"

Version 3: 'House of the Rising Sun'; listen from start to 0'53"

Version 1

(a) **Two** of the following statements are true. **Tick** the **two** statements that you believe to be **true**. **[2 marks]**

Statement	Tick (for true)
The bass guitar plays a scalic idea in the introduction.	
The lead guitar part in the introduction is based on a triplet rhythm pattern.	
A tambourine plays a continuous semiquaver pattern in the verse.	
The chords change on every two beats.	

Listen to **Version 2** and **Version 3** of 'House of the Rising Sun'.

(b) Note **four** ways in which **Version 2** is **different** from the original, **Version 1**.　　　　[4 marks]

Version 2

(i) ....

(ii) ....

(iii) ....

(iv) .... etc.

(c) Note **four** ways in which **Version 3** is **different** from the original, **Version 1**.　　　　[4 marks]

Version 3

(i) ....

(ii) ....

(iii) ....

(iv) ....

(d) Suggest a possible venue for a performance of **Version 2**.　　　　[1 mark]

....

(e) Underline the correct tonality of the music in **Version 1**.　　　　[1 mark]

　　　　Major　　　　　　　　　Pentatonic　　　　　　　　　Minor

WJEC

Listen to **Version 1** and **Version 2** of 'House of the Rising Sun'. In the examination each version will be played **twice**.　　　　**[Total 9 marks]**

Version 1

(a) **Two** of the following statements are true. **Tick** the **two** statements that you believe to be **true**.　　　　[2 marks]

Statement	Tick (for true)
The bass guitar plays a scalic idea in the introduction.	
The lead guitar part in the introduction is based on a triplet rhythm pattern.	
A tambourine plays a continuous semiquaver pattern in the verse.	
The chords change on every two beats.	

Version 2

(b) Now listen to **Version 2** of **'House of the Rising Sun'**.
Tick the box which correctly names the style of music in **Version 2**. **[1 mark]**

Jazz	Fusion	Rock	Folk
☐	☐	☐	☐

(c) Compare the two versions, referring to contrasts in **instrumentation** and any **other features of interest**. When describing **Version 2**, you must concentrate on the **differences** in the music. **[6 marks]**

Version 1	Version 2
Instrumentation:	Instrumentation:
....	....
....	....
....	....
....	....
Other features of interest:	Other features of interest:
....	....
....	....
....	....
....	....

Suggestions to help you identify, explain and describe the use of musical elements

STRUCTURE:
Can you pick out any repetition? How does the music seem to be organised? Can you identify the form?

DYNAMICS:
Is the dynamic loud (forte) or soft (piano)? Are there any contrasts? Does the music get louder (crescendo) or quieter (diminuendo)?

RHYTHM:
Are the note-values basic or complex? Can you hear any syncopation, dotted rhythms or triplets?

MELODY:
Is the melody conjunct or disjunct? Does it include any patterns? Fall into regular or irregular phrases? Any sequences, scales or arpeggios?

TONALITY:
Is the music in a major or minor key? Does it feel as if it changes key/modulates? Is it modal?

HARMONY:
Is the harmony diatonic or dissonant? Can you hear any cadences? Can you pick out any significant chords? Does it feature any other type of scale? Chromatic scale or ideas?

INSTRUMENTS/VOICES:
What types of instruments or voices are used and how? Are there any instrumental or vocal effects you can identify? What types of ensembles or groups are playing or singing?

METRE:
Is the time signature a simple or compound beat? Is it 2/4, 3/4, 4/4 or 6/8? Does it have an irregular beat?

TEMPO:
Is this a fast (allegro), slow (lento) or moderate (moderato) type pace? Are there any changes or contrasts in the pace?

TEXTURE:
Is the texture monophonic, homophonic or polyphonic? Can you pick out any of the following features: unison, chordal, layered, melody and accompaniment, imitation, countermelody?

What exactly does the term 'musical context' mean?

You may have to comment on the 'purpose and intention' of the music	You may have to consider the occasion for which the music has been written, or the venue where it could be performed	You may be asked to comment on something to do with the social, historical or cultural background of the music
Think about: • Why the music was written – was it maybe commissioned for something, or needed for a special purpose (such as Christmas or Easter), or for a film or play? • What sort of atmosphere or mood does the piece have to create?	Think about: • The suitability of the music for the occasion (e.g. celebration, wedding, sad occasion, Easter concert, Remembrance service – the list is endless) • You may be asked to suggest a suitable venue (e.g. church, school, concert hall, rock festival, community gathering, etc.)	Think about: • When the piece may have been written (Baroque, Classical, Romantic, modern eras), and how this has influenced the style • Why the piece may have been composed – perhaps a celebration of something, or an important event, such as a military or royal occasion

 Revision tip

The only time you need to know the exact details for a piece of music will be in relation to the prepared pieces selected for study. Otherwise, you will simply be asked to suggest maybe a mood, venue or occasion – according to how the music feels or what the style is or what it reminds you of.

The marks allocated for such a response are far less than those given for knowledge of the musical elements and language of music. It's nothing to worry about.

CHAPTER 6: MUSICAL TERMS AND THEORY

What Do I Need To Know?

At the back of the GCSE Music specification there is a complete list of musical terms. You are expected to understand what they mean, be able to identify them when appraising, and show understanding of them when performing and composing. Many of them can be found in all the areas of study, some are more specific.

This chapter is intended as a reference section – a bank of necessary musical information for you to consult as and when necessary. It will be of help as you work your way through the course, and also be important revision material before the examination.

Melody (pitch)

Treble clef notes

Bass clef notes

Leger lines are short lines which are added when the music moves beyond the range of the stave.

Intervals

An **interval** in music is not the same as the interval break in a concert or show. It actually means the distance between two notes, i.e. how far apart they are.

For this examination, you need to know the following intervals:

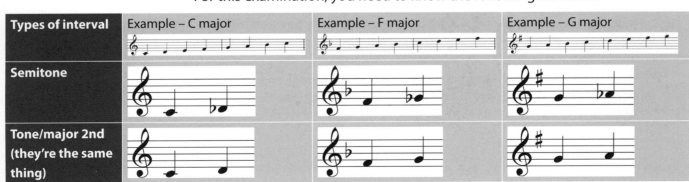

Types of interval	Example – C major	Example – F major	Example – G major
Semitone			
Tone/major 2nd (they're the same thing)			

Revision tip

When you need to work out an interval from looking at a score, think about the lowest note as being the root note of that scale. For example, if the lowest note is D – work the interval out in the key of D major.

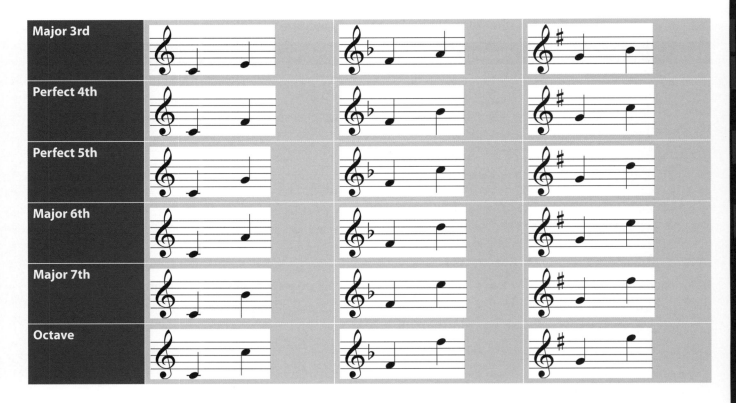

Major 3rd			
Perfect 4th			
Perfect 5th			
Major 6th			
Major 7th			
Octave			

Viola clef

The viola clef is used by the viola in string music, and you will find it used in the extracts set for prepared study. It's also sometimes called the **alto clef**. The middle point of the clef shows the position of middle C. It can be a little confusing to work out, but make sure you understand how to work out the pitches of the notes when studying the prepared extracts.

Notes written in the viola clef	Actual sounds in the treble clef
 The arrows point to the notes that are middle C	

Accidentals

These are signs in the music which show that the pitch of the notes is to be altered.

(#) **Sharp**: Tells you that the note must be raised by a semitone. The note sounds one step (a semitone) higher.

(♭) **Flat**: Tells you that the note must be lowered by a semitone. The note sounds one step (a semitone) lower.

(♮) **Natural**: Cancels out a sharp or flat previously used in the music.

Other terms linked to **melody** include the following.

Term	Meaning
Anacrusis (or up-beat)	A note (or notes) that come before the first strong beat in a passage of music. Sometimes called the 'up-beat' or 'pick-up'. When this happens, the last bar completes the missing beats. **BOOK LINK:** page 24 For example: **Andante** Up-beat/anacrusis – 1 beat (crotchet)　　　　Last bar – 2 beats (minim)
Answering phrase	A second phrase of music, which 'answers' or balances out the first phrase of music.
Anticipation note (WJEC)	When a note of the next chord is played early, preparing for the intended pitch.
Arpeggio/broken chord	When the notes of a chord are played separately and in succession, either ascending or descending. **BOOK LINK:** page 33
Blue notes	The flattened notes in a blues scale.
Chromatic movement	When the melodic movement is in semitones, like part of the chromatic scale.
Conjunct	Stepwise movement in a melodic line, i.e. scalic. **BOOK LINK:** page 31
Contrast	When there is a difference in the music (e.g. melodic contrast, rhythmic contrast, harmonic contrast).
Countermelody	This is an extra melody played the same time as the main theme. **BOOK LINK:** page 72
Disjunct	Angular musical movement that moves in leaps or contains intervals. **BOOK LINK:** page 32
Fanfare	Usually played on brass instruments, this is a loud call to attention, like an announcement. Uses only a few pitches of one or two simple chords. **BOOK LINK:** page 139
High pitch	The higher sounding notes, i.e. treble clef.
Imitation	A contrapuntal device, when a melodic idea (already stated in one part) is copied in another part, while the first tune continues. It may only use the first few notes of the original idea. **BOOK LINK:** page 25
Leitmotif	A musical idea associated with a person, place, object, feeling or idea. **BOOK LINK:** pages 147–149
Low pitch	The lower sounding notes, i.e. bass clef.
Microtone	An interval smaller than a semitone.
Motif	A short music idea, melodic or rhythmic. **BOOK LINK:** page 35
Pentatonic	A five-note scale, commonly used in folk music and found in music all around the world.
Range	Refers to the span of pitches on an instrument or in a piece of music, ranging from the lowest sounding to the highest sounding.
Repetition	When sounds, sequences, melodies, rhythms or sections are repeated. **BOOK LINK:** page 24

Term	Meaning
Scalic	When the musical line moves in steps, just like a scale (i.e. conjunct movement).
Sequence	Repetition of a melodic or harmonic phrase in the same part, but at a higher or lower pitch.
Thematic	The thematic material means the main musical idea – the important melody in a piece of music.
Triadic	Musical movement that uses the notes of a triad.
Trill/ornamentation/decoration	Decorate or embellish the music; can often make it sound 'fussier'. Popular examples of ornaments are trills, mordents and turns.

Rhythm

Note-values

The way that different notes are written on the score tells us how long or short they are, i.e. how long they need to be sung or played. They are partnered with rests for the same values, i.e. how long you need to keep the silence.

Note name	Note symbol and rest symbol	Note-value
Crotchet		1 crotchet beat
Minim		2 crotchet beats
Quaver		½ a crotchet beat
Semibreve		4 crotchet beats
Semiquaver		¼ of a crotchet beat

Time signatures and metre

The time signature in music refers to the numbers found at the start of the music, which tell you how many beats there are in every bar. For this examination you need to know 2/4, 3/4, 4/4 (known as **simple time**) and 6/8 (known as **compound time**).

Simple time	Compound time
The main beat is a crotchet beat.	The main beat is a dotted crotchet beat.
2/4 = 2 crotchet beats in every bar (simple duple)	6/8 = 2 dotted crotchet beats in every bar (compound duple)
3/4 = 3 crotchet beats in every bar (simple triple)	
4/4 = 4 crotchet beats in every bar (simple quadruple)	

Other terms linked to rhythm/metre include the following.

Term	Meaning
Chaal (Eduqas)	This is the dotted rhythm found in bhangra; it is an eight-note rhythmic pattern.
Dance rhythms	Characteristic rhythmic patterns linked with any dance (e.g. waltz, tango, swing, etc.) or the repetitive rhythms and pre-set percussion patterns associated with electronic dance music styles (e.g. house, acid, techno, drum 'n' bass, etc.).
Dotted notes	A dot placed after the note adds half the value of the note again. For example:
Driving rhythms	Rhythms with a relentless energy, moving the music forwards – 'driving' it on.
Irregular metre	When the pattern of beats is more irregular, perhaps made up of two time signatures (e.g. 5/4 time from 3 + 2 beats, alternated).
On the beat	When the notes emphasised are on the strong beats, e.g. the first beat of every bar.
Regular metre	A regular pattern of beats as indicated by the time signature.
Rock rhythms	Typical riffs/rhythms and rhythmic patterns associated with 'rock' music.
Swing rhythms	'Swing' is a type of music that originated in the 1920s/1930s. It involves the unequal performance of notes (e.g. swung quavers) that is characteristic of all types of jazz. It gives a triplet/dotted rhythm feel to the beat – known as a 'swing' rhythm'.
Syncopation/off-beat	Occurs when the strong accents in a bar are shifted. For example, when: • the accent is placed on a normally weak beat • there is a 'rest' sign on the strong beat • a weak beat is 'held' or 'tied' over a strong beat • part of a weak beat is held over to a stronger beat The 'off-beat' is a rhythmic effect where the weak beats are accented, i.e. 'off the beat'. **B🔗OK LINK: page 27**
Tied notes	Two notes of the same pitch, joined together by a short curved line called a tie. For example: The note C is 'tied' over. The first note must be held over for the value of the second note. The second note is not played as a separate note.
Triplet	A rhythmic device where three equal note-values are played in the time of two. For example:

Tonality

Major and minor key signatures (up to four sharps and four flats)

Every major key has a relative minor key, with which it shares the same key signature.

Major keys		Minor keys	Major keys		Minor keys
C major– no sharps or flats		A minor			
Sharp keys			**Flat keys**		
G major	1#	E minor	F major	1♭	D minor
D major	2#	B minor	B♭ major	2♭	G minor
A major	3#	F# minor	E♭ major	3♭	C minor
E major	4#	C# minor	A♭ major	4♭	F minor

Here they are written out for you.

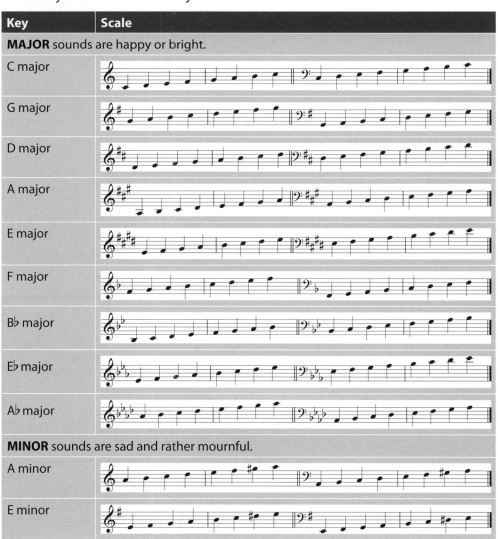

Key	Scale
MAJOR sounds are happy or bright.	
C major	
G major	
D major	
A major	
E major	
F major	
B♭ major	
E♭ major	
A♭ major	
MINOR sounds are sad and rather mournful.	
A minor	
E minor	

Remember

These minor scales are in the harmonic minor form. The melodic minor scales are rather more complex, as they use some different notes when ascending and descending.

Key	Scale
B minor	
F# minor	
C# minor	
D minor	
G minor	
C minor	
F minor	

 Remember

The major pentatonic on G uses notes 1, 2, 3, 5 and 6 of the G major scale.

The minor pentatonic on G uses notes 1, 2, 3, 5 of the natural G minor scale.

Pentatonic scale

- A pentatonic scale is based on just five notes, as shown in the examples below.

- There are two types: the major pentatonic scale and the minor pentatonic scale.

- They are often found in folk or rock music.

G A B D E

G Bb C D F

The **major pentatonic on G** uses notes 1, 2, 3, 5 and 6 of a major scale.

The **minor pentatonic on G** uses notes 1, 3, 4, 5 and 7 of the natural minor scale.

 Get the Grade

Chromatic scale

The chromatic scale is based on all 12 semitones from one note to the note an octave above or below, e.g. from C to C, or G or G. Every step of this scale is a semitone interval – on the keyboard this moves in step, up or down, using every white and black note on the keyboard. Below is the chromatic scale (ascending), starting on C:

Blues scale

This is a scale that flattens the 3rd, 7th and sometimes the 5th note in any major scale. These flattened notes are called 'blue notes'. Below is the blues scale in C:

Modal (Eduqas)

When the description 'modal' is applied to music today, it refers to the 'modes' that evolved from ancient times. A mode is a type of scale, a set of notes. There are seven main categories which have been an important part of musical notation since the Middle Ages. Modes follow different patterns of tones and semitones – and they all have different names. There are major modes, minor modes and modes which are more ambiguous. Modes were often used in church music, and are also found in folk music, blues and jazz music – and are used by guitarists, too.

Some composers use modal passages in their works. In GCSE Music, you don't need to know all the different types of modes, but you might be expected to recognise that a piece of music is modal.

Changing key

The process of changing key in a piece of music is called **MODULATION**. The starting (and ending) key of a piece is called the **HOME KEY**. Sometimes the music passes temporarily throughout another related key – when this happens, we say the music has modulated. This gives a different feeling to the music (sometimes tricky to identify), but is noted in the music by accidentals (flats, sharps and naturals) which clearly do not belong to the home key. Sometimes, accidentals are used just for decoration; however, in this case they are a functional part of the harmony. In GCSE Music you may be asked to identify if modulation has occurred to a related key, such as the dominant or relative minor.

For example:

HOME KEY – C major could modulate to $\Rightarrow$ G major (the dominant)

or $\Rightarrow$ A minor (relative minor)

Harmony

Harmony is created through chords in music. A chord is made when two or more notes are sounded together. If these notes sound good, the harmony is described as **CONSONANT** harmony. If the notes are harsh sounding, or just do not sound good when played together, the harmony is described as **DISSONANT** harmony.

Diatonic harmony

This occurs when TRIADS are built on every note of the scale.

A triad is a chord built up from three notes. For example, following are the triads built on the notes of the C major scale:

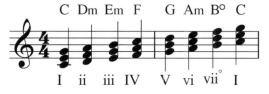

 Remember

Diatonic music is music based on the major and minor scale system.

 Remember

Chromatic harmony is far more complex and includes accidentals not belonging to the home key.

Get the Grade

The dominant 7th chord is formed in C major when an extra note is added to chord V (G ⟹ G7). The chord of V7 is very common, especially at cadence points, e.g. V7 ⟹ I (perfect cadence) is a strong conclusion to a piece of music. Being able to recognise and use this chord correctly may boost your grade.

V^7

Chords I, IV and V are major triads and known as the **primary chords**.

☺ These sound bright and happy.

Chords ii, iii and vi are minor triads and known as the **secondary chords**.

☹ These sound sad.

Chord vii° is a diminished chord. It is also recognised as a secondary chord, but does sound a little different from a major or minor chord; it sounds unfinished – as if it should move on to another chord.

Cadences

A cadence is a rather special progression of two chords in music, and there are four cadences that you must know about for this exam. You will need to recognise how they sound when appraising, and when (and where) they occur in the prepared extracts set for detailed study. If you are able to use them correctly when composing, it will improve the standard of your work.

Type of cadence (F major)	
PERFECT CADENCE 	Uses chords V ⟹ I (dominant ⟹ tonic / C ⟹ F) This cadence sounds complete and finished. It always finishes on the tonic chord. Both chords are major.
IMPERFECT CADENCE 	Lands on chord V (the dominant chord), e.g. I ⟹ V (F ⟹ C) ii ⟹ V (Gm ⟹ C) IV ⟹ V (B♭ ⟹ C) vi ⟹ V (Dm ⟹ C) This cadence sounds incomplete and unfinished. The 2nd chord is always chord V of the key, i.e. the dominant chord, which is major. The chord before may be major or minor.
PLAGAL CADENCE 	Uses chords IV ⟹ I (subdominant ⟹ tonic / B♭ ⟹ F) This cadence also sounds complete and finished. It always finishes on the tonic chord. Both chords are major. It is not such a strong progression as the perfect cadence and is sometimes known as the `Amen' cadence, because it is often found at the end of a hymn.

INTERRUPTED CADENCE	Uses chords V ⇒ vi (dominant ⇒ submediant / C ⇒ Dm).
	This cadence sounds incomplete and unfinished. In a major key, it involves a major chord moving to a minor chord. It is sometimes known as a 'surprise' cadence, because the listener thinks that the dominant chord will resolve to the tonic chord, but it does not, stopping instead on the submediant chord of the key. (In a major key, this will be a minor chord – chord vi; the example shows a D minor chord in F major, which is chord vi in F major. When the home key is a minor key, the submediant chord could actually be major or minor.)

Chord positions

Root position chords

A chord or triad is said to be in root position when the root of the chord is sounded at the lowest point of the chord.

	In the key of C major, all these triads are in root position.

Inversions

Inverted chords and triads are found when other notes of the chord (apart from the root) are heard on the bottom of the chord in the lowest sounding pitch position.

	In the key of C major, all these triads are in first inversion (i.e. the 3rd is in the bass).
	In the key of C major, all the triads are in 2nd inversion (the 5th is in the bass).

> **Remember**
>
> The superscript figure 6 after the chord tells us that the chord is in first inversion. It is a shortened way of writing the figures 6/3 (i.e. the first inversion).
>
> The figures 6/4 after the chord tells us that the chord is in second inversion.

Some other terms linked with harmony

Chord sequence	A series of chords following each other, also known as **harmonic progression**. In a piece of music, the chords sometimes change quickly, perhaps on every beat; at other times, the chords may last for longer, and continue over a number of beats or bars. The rate at which these chords change is known as the **harmonic rhythm**.
Drone	This is a simple harmonic device when one or more notes are held or repeated throughout an extended passage of music.
Harmonic rhythm	The rate at which the harmony changes (i.e. every beat, every two beats, every bar). **BOOK LINK:** page 29
Pedal (pedal note)	A harmonic device where the same note is sustained or repeated, above (or below) which the chords change. **BOOK LINK:** page 29
Power chords	A chord which uses the root and the 5th (i.e. no 3rd). Used by rock guitarists. **BOOK LINK:** pages 186–187

> **Revision tip**
>
> In the prepared extracts selected for analytical study, you must know and understand:
>
> - the home key of the pieces
> - all the key changes (i.e. modulations)
> - all the chords and their positions/inversions
> - where the cadences occur
> - what the cadences are.

Form and structure

Term	Meaning
12-bar blues	A style of blues music with a repeating chord pattern that is 12 bars long. B**OO**K LINK: page 178
32-bar song form	A A B A (with each section being eight bars long). B**OO**K LINK: pages 175–176
Binary form	A two-part structure, i.e. A B (two related sections, both of which may be repeated). B**OO**K LINK: page 16
Break	An instrumental or percussion section that provides a 'break' from the rest of the song or piece. B**OO**K LINK: page 100
Bridge	A piece of music that links two other musical sections together. B**OO**K LINK: page 174
Call and response	A short musical idea (the call) followed by an answering phrase (the response). B**OO**K LINK: page 96
Chorus	A section of a song that has the same words and music when repeated.
Coda	The final section of a movement or piece of music.
Fill	A short musical idea that fills in the 'gaps' in the music at the end of a phrase.
Improvisation	Music that's made up on the spot by the performer.
Introduction	Opening part of a song or piece that 'introduces' the main ideas.
Loop	When a musical idea is 'looped', i.e. repeated indefinitely.
Middle 8	Eight bars in the middle of a song that provide a contrast, i.e. different chord progression. B**OO**K LINK: page 174
Minuet and trio	Often is movement 3 of a symphony or sonata. Both the minuet and the trio are in binary form, each repeated before the minuet returns for a final time, giving an overall ternary form, i.e. A A B B A A. B**OO**K LINK: page 18
Ostinato	A continuously repeated figure or phrase ('obstinately' repeated). B**OO**K LINK: page 27
Outro	The concluding section of a song or piece, i.e. the 'last' part (same as coda). Only used in popular music.
Phrasing – irregular	When the melody is divided up into phrases that are not symmetrically balanced.
Phrasing – regular	When the melody is divided up into shorter, well-balanced and symmetrical phrases. B**OO**K LINK: page 34
Riff	A short, 'catchy' memorable idea or pattern found in jazz, rock or pop; the idea is repeated often in the music. B**OO**K LINK: page 187
Rondo form	A recurring section (A) with alternating 'episodes', i.e. A B A C A. B**OO**K LINK: page 19
Strophic	This structure has verses that are musically the same each time. Only the lyrics change. B**OO**K LINK: page 21
Ternary form	A three-part structure, i.e. A B A (the final section may be an exact or a varied repeat of the first section). B**OO**K LINK: page 17

Term	Meaning
Theme and variations	The theme is a melody (either original or borrowed) and a number of variations are created – sometimes simply decorated, sometimes more complex. BOOK LINK: page 20
Verse	A section of a song that has the same music when repeated but different lyrics each time.

Texture

Term	Meaning
2-, 3- or 4-part textures	Music written for 2-, 3- or 4-part voices or instruments.
Alberti bass	A type of accompaniment figure that uses broken chords. BOOK LINK: page 34
Canon	A compositional device where a melody in one part is repeated exactly after the other, usually with some overlapping. BOOK LINK: page 71
Chordal	When the style of the music is delivered through the harmony, i.e. the interest is vertical, and in the chords more than the melody. BOOK LINK: pages 68–69
Countermelody	A new melody, combined with a melody that has been heard previously. BOOK LINK: page 72
Descant	A decorative melodic line, higher in pitch than the main melody in a piece of vocal music, e.g. in a hymn, Christmas carol or similar vocal piece.
Drone	Constantly repeated or sustained note(s). A drone with two notes usually consists of the tonic and the dominant notes (often associated with folk music). BOOK LINK: page 29
Homophonic	A melody + accompaniment texture. BOOK LINK: page 145
Imitation	This happens when the melodic idea presented in one part is stated immediately after in another part, i.e. where one part 'copies' another. BOOK LINK: page 25
Layered	When several layers of sounds or musical lines are combined to build up the texture. BOOK LINK: page 69
Melody and accompaniment	When the melody or theme is the main feature, and the other parts support, i.e. 'accompany', the melody. BOOK LINK: pages 70–71
Monophonic	Music in which there is a single line, whether for a soloist or for unison voices or instruments. BOOK LINK: page 145
Polyphonic	Two or more melodies, equally as important, played together. (The same as counterpoint.) BOOK LINK: page 145
Round	A short vocal canon for unaccompanied singing (e.g. *London's Burning*, *Three Blind Mice*). BOOK LINK: pages 62–63
Stab chords	'Staccato' (short) chord(s) that add dramatic impact in a piece of music. Usually lasts for one beat and played by horns/brass instruments. Found in various types of music, e.g. jazz and rock.
Unison	When voices/instruments are playing at the same pitch, i.e. all parts sounding the same note. BOOK LINK: page 68
Walking bass	Type of bass part that is continually moving along. The notes are all on the beat and the movement is mainly by step. BOOK LINK: pages 101–102

Tempo

The tempo of the music means the **speed** of the beat. There are different terms used in music to state the tempo of a piece, but the following are the ones that you must know.

Term	Meaning
Accelerando (*Accel.*)	Gradually increasing the speed
Adagio/Lento	Slowly, leisurely
Allegretto	Moderately fast, slower than allegro
Allegro/Vivace	Lively, brisk, rapid
Moderato/Andante	At a moderate speed/a 'walking speed' – not too slow
Pause	A pause sign is a symbol which means that the note should be held longer than the original value
Ritardando/Rallentando (*Rit./Rall.*)	Slowing down
Rubato	A 'freer' approach to the tempo; when the performer gives an expressive interpretation of the music – not sticking strictly to time, but without altering the overall pace

Get the Grade

Some other useful terms:
- A tempo – in the original tempo
- Largo – very slow
- Presto – very quick
- Ritenuto – in slower time

Dynamics

The dynamics in music tell the performers how **loudly** or **softly** to play. The following terms are the ones that you need to know.

Term	Meaning
Crescendo (*cresc.*)	Getting louder; gradually increasing in loudness
Diminuendo (*dim.*)	Getting quieter; gradually decreasing in loudness
Forte (*f*)	Loud
Fortissimo (*ff*)	Very loud
Mezzo forte (*mf*)	Moderately loud
Mezzo piano (*mp*)	Moderately soft
Pianissimo (*pp*)	Very softly, very quietly
Piano (*p*)	Softly, quietly
Sforzando (*sf*)	With force; a sudden emphasis

☑ Get the Grade

Two useful signs to know:

gradually getting louder ⟶ gradually getting softer

p ⟶ *f* ⟶ *p*

crescendo (*cresc.*)   decrescendo (*decresc.*)
or diminuendo (*dim.*)

Musical styles

These are the different types of music and styles you have studied throughout the GCSE Music course.

Term	Meaning
Ballad	A type of song which tells a story (in rock or pop music, this is usually a love story).
Baroque	Music typical of the period from about 1600–1750. BOOK LINK: page 12
Bhangra (Eduqas)	Fusion of traditional Indian/Pakistani music with modern club dance music. BOOK LINK: pages 190–194
Blues	A genre of music originating from American negro spirituals; important features include the 12-bar structure, 'blue notes', blues scale. Generally has a mood of sadness. BOOK LINK: pages 93–97
Cerdd dant (WJEC)	This is the art of vocal improvisation over a traditional Welsh folk tune. BOOK LINK: pages 113–114
Chamber music	Music intended for a small group of performers, regarded as soloists on equal terms; music intended for domestic performance with one instrument per part. BOOK LINK: pages 74–84
Classical	Music typical of the period between about 1750–1810. BOOK LINK: page 13
Film music	Music written especially for the screen, including underscore and thematic music that engages with the storyline and characters. BOOK LINK: pages 116–132
Fusion	Music in which two or more styles are blended (e.g. pop and Classical). BOOK LINK: pages 188–190
Hip-hop	Style of rap originating in the 1980s, which added 'scratching' onto records.
Jazz	A genre of music originating from New Orleans which now has many types of styles; important features include syncopation, improvisation and interesting often complex harmonies. BOOK LINK: pages 93–94, 98–106
Minimalism	A 20th-century genre, characterised by the subtle varied repetition of simple melodic, rhythm or harmonic ideas (or cells). BOOK LINK: page 150
Musical theatre/musical	A musical play or drama in which singing, acting and dance play an important part. BOOK LINK: pages 84–92
Pop	A genre of music that originated in the USA and the UK in the mid-1950s. It uses ideas and musical elements from many different styles.
Reggae	A style of music originating from the West Indies, popular in the 1970s. BOOK LINK: page 166
Rock	Originated in the USA as 'rock and roll' in the mid-1950s. BOOK LINK: pages 162–173
Romantic	Music typical of the period between about 1810–1910. BOOK LINK: page 13

Term	Meaning
Soul	A form of black music originating from the 1970s, influenced by gospel music.
Welsh folk (WJEC)	The type of music influenced by the national heritage of Wales – the distinctive instruments, folk tunes and singing. **BOOK LINK: pages 107–115**
Western Classical Tradition	Means music written between about 1650–1910. **BOOK LINK: pages 12–13**

Sonority

Sonority in music is all about the type of sound – the resonance and the timbre. You must know about the following.

Instruments, voices and groupings	
Acoustic	• To do with sound as it is heard; the sound quality in a room or building. • Musical instruments whose sound is not electronically generated through an amplifier.
Basso continuo	The name given to the continuous bass line in Baroque music often played by the harpsichord and the cello. **BOOK LINK: pages 73–74**
Brass	Trumpet, French horn, trombone, tuba.
Dohl (Eduqas)	The drum used in traditional bhangra. **BOOK LINK: page 191**
Groupings	Solo, duet, trio, quartet.
Guitars	Classical or Spanish guitar, electric guitar, bass guitar.
Keyboards	Synthesiser, piano, organ, harpsichord.
Orchestra	Large instrumental ensemble which has four families of instruments: string, woodwind, brass and percussion.
Percussion	Tuned: timpani, glockenspiel, xylophone. Untuned: drum kit, snare drum, cymbal, hand-held percussion.
Pop/rock group	Small ensemble that performs rock/pop music. A common line-up would be lead guitar, rhythm guitar (one or both also doing vocals), bass guitar and drummer.
Rhythm section	Part of a pop or jazz group that supplies the rhythm, i.e. bass, drums and guitar/keyboard (playing the chords).
Sarangi (Eduqas)	Small Indian string instrument, with no frets. **BOOK LINK: page 191**
Sitar (Eduqas)	Large Indian string instrument with a long neck and frets. **BOOK LINK: page 191**
String quartet	Group of four string instruments – two violins, a viola and a cello.
Strings	Violin, viola, cello, double bass (and harp).
Tabla (Eduqas)	Pair of drums used in Indian classical music (called the dayan and the bayan) **BOOK LINK: page 190**
Tumbi (Eduqas)	Single string Indian instrument, plucked; associated with the folk music of Punjab, and popular in Western bhangra music. **BOOK LINK: page 191**
Woodwind	Flute, oboe, clarinet, bassoon (and saxophone, which is not an orchestral instrument).

Voices	
A cappella	Singing without any instrumental backing or accompaniment.
Backing vocals	Singers who provide vocal harmony or countermelodies for the lead vocalist.
Chorus	• Section of a song or hymn. • A vocal ensemble in a musical, opera or oratorio.
Female voices	Soprano, alto (mezzo-soprano).
Male voices	Tenor, bass (baritone).
Technology	
Echo	The repetition of a musical phrase (or sound) that has less impact and volume than the original phrase or sound.
Panning	The distribution of a sound signal into a multi-channel sound field. The panning control adjusts the sound through the left and right speakers.
Phasing	A delay effect in music technology.
Reverb	An effect that adds an echo to the sound. It can be used on most amplified instruments and also voices.
Sampler	An electronic device for storing and altering sounds.
Synthesised/electronic	• An electronic keyboard with different sounds. • A type of music that uses electronic devices to produce and alter sounds.
Performance techniques/articulation	
Accent	Additional stress or emphasis placed on a particular note.
Arco	The instruction for string players to play their instrument using the bow.
Belt	The lower, more powerful part of the voice range.
Detached	A type of musical articulation which describes notes that have been shortened (i.e. staccato).
Distortion	An effect for guitar players that distorts the note.
Divisi	The instruction in music for orchestral players reading the same musical staff to divide into two or more parts.
Double stopping	When a string instrument plays two notes at the same time.
Drum roll	A performance technique for drums that involves a rapid succession of beats. A drum roll is often used to build anticipation in the music.
Falsetto	Male vocal technique used to extend the voice into a higher range than usual.
Glissando	A slide from one pitch to another.

Performance techniques/articulation

Hammer on	A performance technique for a string instrument with frets, such as the guitar. It occurs when the guitarist brings his finger down sharply on the fretboard (behind a fret), causing a note to sound. (This technique is the opposite of the 'pull-off', where the finger on the fret is released after the note has been struck.)
Humming	A vocal sound produced with the mouth closed.
Legato	An instruction for the music to be played smoothly.
Melismatic	Vocal music where a syllable of the text has been set to a number of different notes.
Muted	A 'muted' effect is achieved when mutes are used to dampen or quieten the sound of string or brass instruments.
Pitch bend	When a performer changes the pitch of the note by a very small amount (e.g. using the facility on a synthesiser).
Pizzicato	'Plucked' (i.e. way of playing a string instrument).
Plucked	A way of pulling and releasing the string quickly on a string instrument to produce the sound (i.e. pizzicato).
Rap	A type of pop music originating from the USA where the words are spoken quickly and rhythmically against an instrumental backing.
Rim-shot	A performance technique for percussion, when the sound is produced by hitting the rim and head of a drum with a drum stick at the same time.
Scat	A style of singing in jazz music that is improvised, and where the voice is used in imitation of an instrument (i.e. no words, or using nonsense words).
Slap bass	A performance technique for bass guitar (or double bass) by bouncing strings against the fret board to achieve a 'percussive' sound.
Slurred	A style of playing two or more notes smoothly: joined with a 'slur' (legato).
Staccato	Detached notes, shorter than their full length.
Sustained	Held on, i.e. a sustained note = a held note.
Syllabic	Vocal music where each syllable of the text has been set to a different note.
Tongued	A performance technique used by wind instruments to define different notes (i.e. separating notes by stopping the airflow with the tongue).
Tremolo	Rapid bowing on a string instrument to produce a dramatic effect.
Vibrato	A rapid, slight variation in pitch when singing or playing some musical instruments, which produces a stronger or richer tone.

Features to look out for when explaining and describing the musical elements.

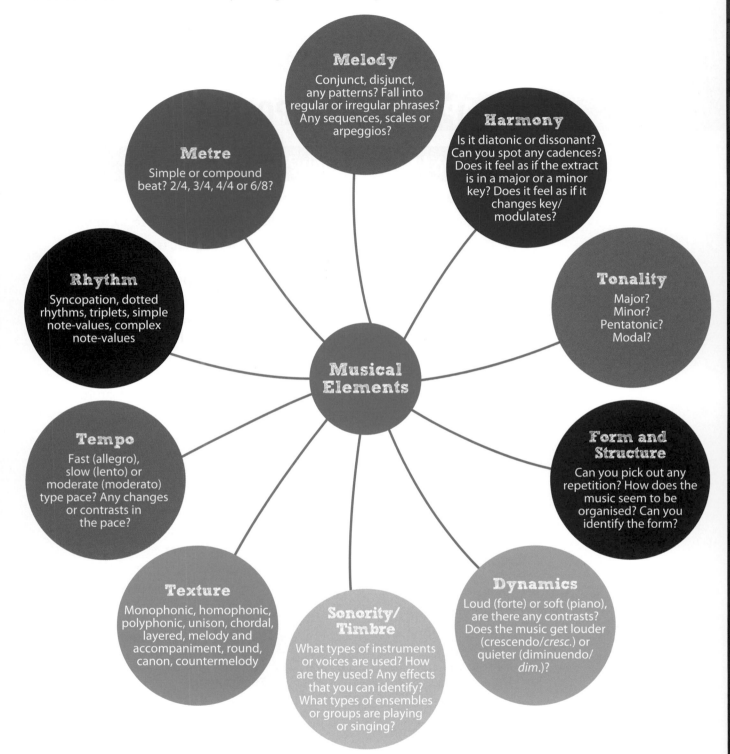

Melody
Conjunct, disjunct, any patterns? Fall into regular or irregular phrases? Any sequences, scales or arpeggios?

Metre
Simple or compound beat? 2/4, 3/4, 4/4 or 6/8?

Harmony
Is it diatonic or dissonant? Can you spot any cadences? Does it feel as if the extract is in a major or a minor key? Does it feel as if it changes key/modulates?

Rhythm
Syncopation, dotted rhythms, triplets, simple note-values, complex note-values

Tonality
Major? Minor? Pentatonic? Modal?

Musical Elements

Tempo
Fast (allegro), slow (lento) or moderate (moderato) type pace? Any changes or contrasts in the pace?

Form and Structure
Can you pick out any repetition? How does the music seem to be organised? Can you identify the form?

Texture
Monophonic, homophonic, polyphonic, unison, chordal, layered, melody and accompaniment, round, canon, countermelody

Sonority/Timbre
What types of instruments or voices are used? How are they used? Any effects that you can identify? What types of ensembles or groups are playing or singing?

Dynamics
Loud (forte) or soft (piano), are there any contrasts? Does the music get louder (crescendo/*cresc.*) or quieter (diminuendo/*dim.*)?

SECTION 2
COMPOSING AND PERFORMING

CHAPTER 7: COMPOSING

What Do I Need To Know?

▸ You must complete **two** compositions.

▸ Your completed coursework portfolio should last three to six minutes.

▸ One composition must be in response to a set brief, issued by the exam board at the start of the year in which you will complete the examination. There will be a choice of four (one per area of study) and you need to select one.

▸ The second composition is a free composition, for which you must set your own brief. You can link it to an area of study if you wish.

Obviously, showing your musical understanding and use of the musical elements applies to all areas of study. However, there are certain features that have been identified with the different areas of study which you should consider.

Musical forms and devices
Think about:

Forms: structures, e.g. binary, ternary, minuet and trio, rondo, variation and strophic

A sense of balance and proportion

Devices: e.g. contrast, imitation, sequence, ostinato, syncopation, pedal notes, canon, melodic and rhythmic motifs, chord progressions cadences and modulations

Music for ensemble
Think about:

The genres:

• **Chamber music**

• **Musical theatre**

• **Jazz and blues**

Groupings: e.g. jazz trio, string quartet, vocal duet/trio, blues group

Textures: e.g. monophonic, homophonic, polyphonic, unison, layered, melody and accompaniment, countermelody, canon

Film music
Think about:

• **Timbre**

• **Tone-colour**

• **Dynamics**

Devices: e.g. creating a mood, use of leitmotifs, use of dynamics and contrast for special effects, use of minimalistic techniques, layering, distinctive and strong thematic material, transformation of themes to reflect the mood and situation

Popular music
Think about:

Structures: 32-bar song form, middle 8, bridge, instrumental break, introduction, verse chorus, outros, use of hook, etc.

Instrumentation: bass lines, drum kit/percussion, guitar styles, keyboard parts, lead and backing singers, front-line instruments

Devices: e.g. riffs, chords and progressions, contrast, layering, cadences, driving rhythms, syncopation, close harmony work, improvisation, walking bass

How to achieve your best work in composing

You may associate the word 'revision' with the study of written work for the listening exam, and not so much with your coursework. But you can certainly also 'revise' with regard to the composing portfolio.

Completing two compositions will take a lot of thought and careful planning. Many students are so pleased and relieved to complete their pieces that they do not want to change anything, make improvements, or act on any advice suggested or further guidance given by the teachers.

However, this is the key to success. Composers from both the past and present edit and change their ideas as they refine their work and continue to develop the musical ideas – many are never truly satisfied with the outcome.

This section of the book is intended to help you focus on the exact requirements of this part of the course: a reminder of what is required to ensure good marks.

Musical forms and devices

Music for ensemble

Film music

Popular music

BOOK LINK: pages 230–239

 Remember

A definition of 'revise' is to amend or alter: to revise one's opinion, to alter something ... in order to make corrections, improve or update.

 Get the Grade

Always plan a timetable and stick to it. Leave sufficient time to consider what you have written. Judge the quality of your initial ideas and, in the light of any judgement and with teacher guidance, refine and amend your work, making sure that you have developed the material.

Your target is to score well in the assessment grid, which identifies the level of your achievement in three ways:

Creativity and development of musical ideas	Technical control of musical elements and resources	Structure and stylistic coherence
This assesses: • the quality of your basic material • how you develop the ideas • how effective the contrasts of tone, colour and mood are	This assesses: • your choice of elements and resources • your use and control of a variety of musical elements (including technology)	This assesses: • your organisation and presentation of the ideas • the response to the given brief • how effective the final outcome is

Responding to the brief

The starting point is always the brief, whether it is the one that you have selected out of the choice of four given by the exam board, or the brief that you have decided on for the free composition.

Planning

- Think about your initial response to the brief: the audience or occasion, the area of study, the instruments/voices, and how you will record or store your musical ideas.

- Consider the contrasts: what could they be? What 'moods' are you aiming for? How could they be organised? How will they be varied?

- How are you going to use and present the musical elements? Making good choices needs careful consideration and application – demonstrating control over the musical elements is the key to achieving higher marks.

The content

- The first thing to do is **create** your initial musical ideas, i.e. the first section of your piece. You need to think about the melodic and rhythmic content, chord progressions and so on. Make sure that these effectively reflect the chosen brief and achieve the opening mood through appropriate tone colours, suitable dynamics, tempo and careful arrangement of the ideas for instruments/voices.

- The second stage is to **plan** how these ideas will be contrasted, e.g. a new melody? A different key? By varying the texture? By creating a different 'mood'? Consider what change of elements is necessary to create a contrast of mood.

- The third stage is to **develop** the initial material.

- The final – very important – stage is to **refine your work. Improve the weaker areas and alter what needs to be altered**.

Remember

Re-visit and revise – rearrange if necessary.

Creating musical ideas: understanding chords and melodies

There is no one way to compose; everyone will work differently. Some students will compose their melodies first, then add the chords and accompaniment; others will plan the harmonic outline first and then create the theme. Whichever way you think works best for you, over the duration of the GCSE Music course you will have come up with ideas, and hopefully thought about expanding and developing those ideas. It's all about how you put the elements together to get the result you want – one that creates and combines the elements to achieve an effective sense of style and character in response to your chosen brief.

Melody

The ideas	How to show control
✓ Compose some short motifs that are 'tuneful' ✓ Include conjunct movement and some intervals ✓ You could also include arpeggio ideas, some rests or syncopation (if appropriate)	✓ Create questions and answering phrases ✓ Balance the ideas: repeat when necessary, include contrast when change is needed

The ideas	How to show control
✓ Listen to the completed melody – without any accompaniment. Pinpoint any notes that sound incorrect and change them ✓ Make sure your main idea is not too complex (then you can develop the ideas later) ✓ Be critical. Is it a good tune? Is it memorable? Be satisfied before moving on	✓ Think about the shape the melody makes: 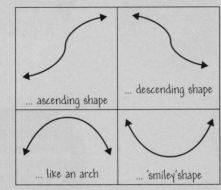 ✓ Organise the ideas into a structure (e.g. A A B A, A B A B, A B A, etc.) ✓ Have a 'high' point and a 'low' point in the melody

 Get the Grade

- Don't use a melody (or part of a melody) that is already 'famous' or well-known ... compose your own.

- The melody has to have character, direction, shape and balance ... it is not just a random collection of notes. For the best grade, it needs to 'travel' ... and make sense musically.

Chords

The ideas	How to show control
✓ Compose various short progressions of chords ✓ Think about working within a key (if appropriate) ✓ Play pitches together to create chords that you feel suit the piece – don't always start and stop with C major ✓ Build up a chord sequence by starting with one chord of three notes, then change one note at a time (or add, or take away a note) ✓ Listen to the ideas. Pinpoint anything that does not sound correct and change it	✓ Establish the sense of the 'home' key ✓ Work out the way to move to a related key ✓ Repeat the strongest progressions as necessary but always include some contrasting sections – ring the changes ✓ Think about phrase endings and cadences ✓ Avoid using chords in root position all the time – experiment with inversions and 7ths ✓ Even when the harmony is more dissonant, control the selection and contrast of the content

Rhythm

The ideas	How to show control
✓ Use more simple note-values to start – this gives opportunity for development later on ✓ Strong rhythmic patterns help to establish identity and character – so spend time on these ✓ Tap out or play the rhythmic ideas you want before recording or notating ✓ Work within a clearly established time signature before adding variety	✓ Decide on the main rhythmic patterns and organise them thoughtfully ✓ Don't change the time signature too often in one piece ✓ Include a variety of rhythms when developing your ideas to show your understanding, e.g. syncopation, triplets, dotted rhythms, rests, semiquaver patterns, accented notes ✓ Don't fit patterns together in a random way; this shows a lack of control. Plan and balance the ideas

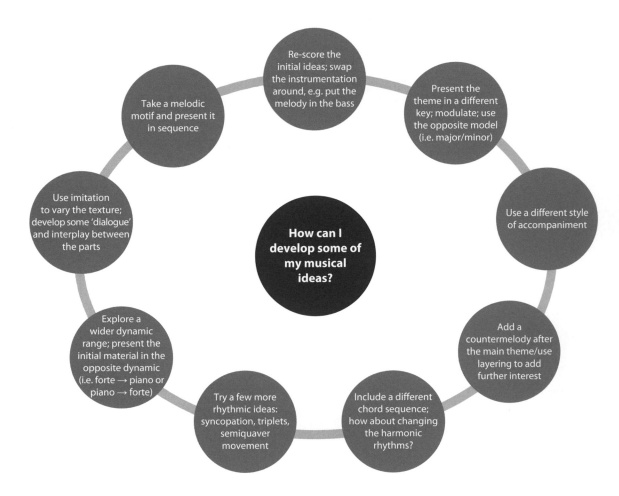

✅ Get the Grade

Some extended knowledge

Impress by using devices such as augmentation, diminution and inversion to develop the melody.

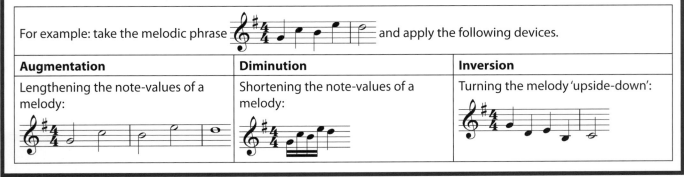

Augmentation	Diminution	Inversion
Lengthening the note-values of a melody:	Shortening the note-values of a melody:	Turning the melody 'upside-down':

Checklist – your composition should include:

✓ A carefully organised structure.

✓ A well-balanced melody, with clear phrases.

✓ Accompaniment patterns that support the melodic line.

✓ Convincing chord progressions (with cadences as appropriate).

✓ Interesting use of patterns and devices.

✓ A variety of musical elements to obtain contrasting colours and moods.

✓ Development of ideas using a variety of compositional devices.

✓ Refinement of the initial ideas.

Completing the candidate log

Many candidates ask for advice when completing the candidate log. In the first section, you will just need to complete the necessary examination information, explaining details of the recording process. The following three sections need to be completed in some detail – hopefully these suggestions will help.

 Remember

You should download the candidate log from the WJEC/Eduqas website as a Word document. You can then add details as you go along, which will make things much easier for you.

SUPERVISION AND MONITORING

The following three sections are to be completed by the candidate and countersigned by the teacher during the composition process to show development and progress.

FIRST DRAFT: Initial ideas (explain how you began your composition)

- ✓ Give reasons for choice of brief.
- ✓ What are your first ideas? Outline your initial thoughts and plans.
- ✓ What has influenced and inspired you?
- ✓ What musical elements and features are you going to use – and how?
- ✓ Explain your choices: why your ideas are a suitable response to the brief/how they reflect the area of study.
- ✓ Outline the process so far – exactly what have you completed?
- ✓ Give details of teacher guidance and advice, and what targets have been set.

Subject teacher: .... Date: ....

SECOND DRAFT: Extension and development (explain how you developed your original ideas)

- ✓ Outline your plans mid-stage: what overall structure you have decided upon and how you plan to use the musical elements to achieve contrast.
- ✓ How are you going to develop your ideas? Mention any changes in texture, key, melody, rhythm or harmonies. What devices are you going to use (e.g. imitation, sequence, layering, counterpoint, etc.)?
- ✓ Have you any further thoughts about the brief or reflection on the area of study, which have had a further effect on the musical content?
- ✓ Give details of teacher advice, what targets have been achieved and what new targets have been set.

Subject teacher: .... Date: ....

FINAL SUBMISSION: Completion (explain how you finalised your piece, including details of the software, auto accompaniments, etc. used in the final recording).

- ✓ What finishing touches have you added to your piece?
- ✓ What software (if any) have you used? How do you think this benefitted the piece and your work?
- ✓ Have you used any musical ideas that are not your own? Any non-original material must be acknowledged and its use explained (e.g. drum loops, sampled sounds or patterns, programmed accompaniments, etc.).
- ✓ How do you feel you have responded to advice and reached the targets that have been set?
- ✓ Have you achieved what you set out to do? Have you fulfilled the brief? What do you think is particularly successful about your piece?

Subject teacher: .... Date: ....

Make sure all sections include your teacher's signature and have been dated.

Scores and lead sheets

Many students are able to present fully completed scores with their compositions, either by using a program such as Sibelius, or by transferring their music (via midi) to a program like this in order to realise the musical score. There are many different programs available for your use.

When such a score has been submitted, you do not need to include any kind of analysis of the music in the candidate log.

If it is not possible for you to create a notated score, then you must include what is known as a lead sheet. In a lead sheet you need to describe the actual content of the music and explain exactly what you have included in the composition. The lead sheet is required in addition to the candidate log.

What should I include on a lead sheet?

 Revision tip

Include performance directions such as dynamics and tempo markings on the score/lead sheet. This shows that you are thinking about control of the musical elements.

Information about the tempo, dynamics and texture

A structural outline showing the overall form

Lyrics (if it is a song), including the melodic notation if possible

Details of the harmony, melody and rhythm

The lead sheet

Details of all composition devices (e.g. sequence, imitation, layering, etc.)

Explanation of what instruments/voices have been used and how

✅ Get the Grade

- If you have used technology to record your ideas, you may be able to access an editing window, which would provide you with snippets of notation that you could include to support the presentation of your music.

- There is no requirement for notation **if you perform all parts yourself**. Just an explanation of the musical content is perfectly sufficient.

Annotated screenshot

This is an example of a typical screenshot, annotated with boxes that contain explanations of the musical content. Information presented by many GCSE Music students is often linked to instrumental features and compositional devices.

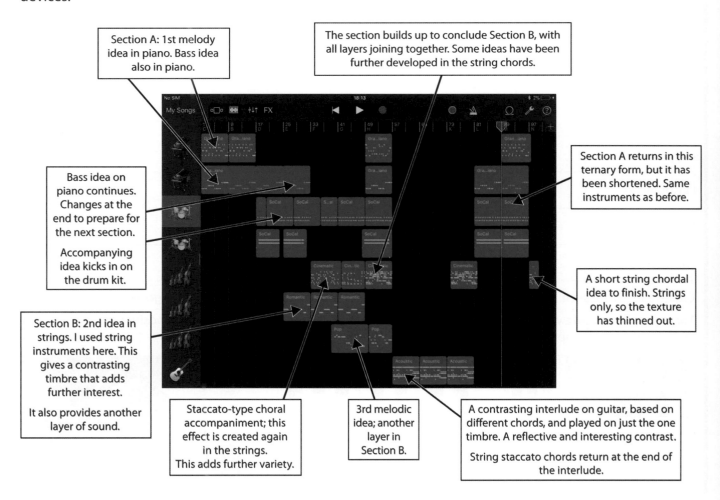

Section A: 1st melody idea in piano. Bass idea also in piano.

The section builds up to conclude Section B, with all layers joining together. Some ideas have been further developed in the string chords.

Bass idea on piano continues. Changes at the end to prepare for the next section.

Accompanying idea kicks in on the drum kit.

Section A returns in this ternary form, but it has been shortened. Same instruments as before.

Section B: 2nd idea in strings. I used string instruments here. This gives a contrasting timbre that adds further interest.

It also provides another layer of sound.

A short string chordal idea to finish. Strings only, so the texture has thinned out.

Staccato-type choral accompaniment; this effect is created again in the strings. This adds further variety.

3rd melodic idea; another layer in Section B.

A contrasting interlude on guitar, based on different chords, and played on just the one timbre. A reflective and interesting contrast.

String staccato chords return at the end of the interlude.

IMPORTANT! What is often omitted with such an outline are sufficient details about the melody, rhythms, harmonies (including your choice of inversions), tonality, tempo and dynamics.

What is also perhaps missing in the annotation above is sufficient explanation. For example:

- At the opening, layers were added – what were the musical ideas in these layers?

- It states that string instruments were used – but the composer could be more specific – any particular string instruments? What type of musical material were they given exactly?

- It says 'ideas were developed'. It is always best to say how the ideas were developed, and name any devices used in their development.

☑ Get the Grade

To ensure that you get credit for all your ideas, make sure you explain fully what you have included. You could present such information in a table. For example, if your piece was in rondo form, you could present the necessary information as follows:

	Section A	Section B	Section A	Section C	Section A
Melody					
Rhythm					
Tempo					
Dynamics					
Instruments					
Harmony					
[Lyrics]					

Create a template such as this in a Word doc. You can then complete a little at a time as you go along.

Tip: If you are not sure what chords you have used, take a picture of the guitar or keyboard positioning and include that. For example, see the photos below.

BOOK LINK:
pages 240–243

Writing an evaluation (WJEC)

If you are following the GCSE Music course for Wales, you must write an evaluation of the piece composed in response to the brief set by the WJEC. You will have selected out of a choice of four.

When you evaluate something, you are making a judgement about it. You must look at the composition as a whole and think about its successes and weaknesses.

To gain top marks, you must give an 'in-depth' evaluation which shows *perceptive critical judgement*, and when writing you must use *accurate music terminology*. You are required to provide a detailed account, which must be between 500 and 1,000 words. Every sentence needs to be relevant, and you need to consider carefully what needs to be included. Explain **why** specific decisions have been made.

1 Give details of the selected brief.

[**Example WJEC brief**: Compose a piece of folk dance music for the Eisteddfod competition. You must write for at least two instruments (of your own choice).]

2 How does the composition fulfil the set brief?

Give reasons why you chose this particular brief.

What research did you do? What pieces of music did you listen to for inspiration? Why were they suitable for this brief?

Was there anything you wished that you had explored further?

How did you organise and plan your approach? What were your main targets?

Was there a meaning or mood that you wanted to convey? Why? Have you managed to achieve that?

What things were the most important considerations when you were thinking about fulfilling the brief?

What advice did you received from the teacher in the initial stages?

3 How were musical elements used in the piece?

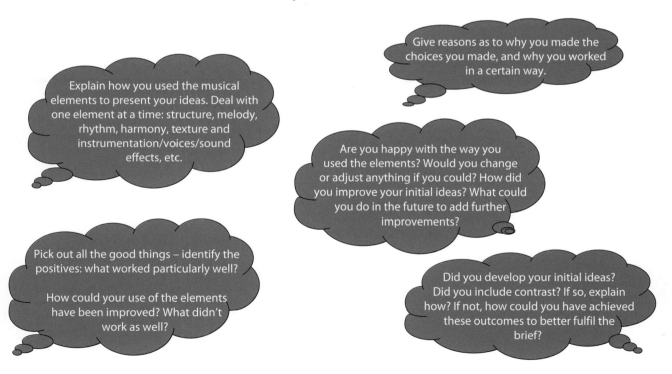

Give reasons as to why you made the choices you made, and why you worked in a certain way.

Explain how you used the musical elements to present your ideas. Deal with one element at a time: structure, melody, rhythm, harmony, texture and instrumentation/voices/sound effects, etc.

Are you happy with the way you used the elements? Would you change or adjust anything if you could? How did you improve your initial ideas? What could you do in the future to add further improvements?

Pick out all the good things – identify the positives: what worked particularly well?

How could your use of the elements have been improved? What didn't work as well?

Did you develop your initial ideas? Did you include contrast? If so, explain how? If not, how could you have achieved these outcomes to better fulfil the brief?

4 How effective was the completed composition?

Did you achieve what you set out to do? Are you happy with the outcome? Does it successfully meet the brief? How?

Did your skills improve during the composing process? How did this help in the composing process?

What were other people's opinions of your piece?

How effective was the completed composition? Give reasons for your response.

Are the musical ideas clearly balanced? Is the content interesting? What were you pleased with?

Did you make the best use of ICT? What was the quality of the final recording like?

What further improvements would you make if you had more time?

Do you think that you have shown technical control of the resources and musical elements? How?

Remember

Your TEACHER can see one draft, but must not provide any written feedback. You will be given general advice, but not specific suggestions on how to improve the content.

Finally, the evaluation will be authenticated by the teacher to confirm that it is all your own work.

CHAPTER 8: PERFORMING

What Do I Need To Know?

▶ **You need to perform a minimum of two pieces.**

▶ **The standard level required is broadly equivalent to grade 3 of the graded music examinations.**

▶ **You need to perform for four to six minutes.**

▶ **One of your pieces must be an ensemble piece, which must last for at least a minute.**

▶ **The other piece(s) may be solo or ensemble.**

▶ **One piece must link to an area of study** [WJEC: you must produce a programme note to accompany this].

▶ **You must present a score or lead sheet for every piece that you perform.**

WJEC

Remember: Time your pieces.

• If your performance lasts for less than four minutes, there will be a **penalty of 5 marks**.

• If your performance lasts for less than three-and-a-half minutes you will score **ZERO**.

Eduqas

Remember: Time your pieces,

• If your performance lasts for less than four minutes you will score **ZERO**.

Music is a performing art. For many, the enjoyment of performing is the very reason for choosing this course; for others, performing may be a little more daunting. During your GCSE Music course you will have been encouraged by your teacher to perform as much as possible – in class, on your own and in groups (both small and large).

Your targets are:

• to improve your practical technique and become more skilful

• to improve your ability to communicate through your music

• to take advantage of every opportunity to perform with and in front of others.

You know that you have to practise your pieces – but remember that you also need to practise performing. It's not just about getting all the notes in the right place at the right time. To obtain top marks, you need to perform with feeling and fluency, with sensitivity and confidence, always paying attention to performance directions.

Your teacher will record and assess your performances, and they will need to keep a copy of the score or lead sheet. A sample of the work from your GCSE Music class will be sent to the exam board for moderation, and your work could well be included in this sample.

Selecting music for performance

You must choose the music for performance very carefully. The content has to be suitable; take advice from your class teacher, and your private or peripatetic music tutor. The important thing is that these teachers know the assessment criteria, which are the requirements and the standards against which you will be judged.

If you are a 'pop' musician, you may want to perform your favourite songs, but the GCSE Music practical assessment may not be the best place to do this. Players of an orchestral instrument, or pianists, frequently choose pieces that are too difficult; performing a simpler piece may well result in higher marks.

The level of difficulty

The GCSE Music performing standard is broadly equivalent to grade 3 of the graded music examinations.

Remember

If you perform a piece of music below the grade 3 standard, it will be considered as 'easier than standard level' and some marks will be deducted.

If you perform a piece of music above the grade 3 standard, it will be considered as 'more difficult than standard level' and some marks will be added.

The assessment grid containing the assessment criteria is included in the GCSE Music specification document, available online or from your teacher.

 Get the Grade

> You will achieve your best marks when you select a piece at the correct level for you.
>
> You will be assessed on:
>
>
>
> **Accuracy**
> **Technical control**
> **Expression and interpretation**
>
>
>
> The best tip you can be given is: don't choose pieces that are too ambitious. It is better to offer pieces that you can perform to a very good level, to show technical and expressive understanding, than deliver an average performance of a piece that is clearly too demanding for you. If you have considered playing a piece that has 'tricky' challenges – think twice. These 'challenges' are the very sections that will trip you up on the day.
>
> The assessor cannot award marks for a candidate being prepared to 'have a go' – it's really not about what your potential ability may be. You will get credit for what you have performed, not on your potential or what might have been on a good day.

Linking one piece to an area of study

You can link any of your pieces to one of the areas of study. It could be a solo piece or the ensemble piece. You can choose any of the four areas of study – it's up to you. Some examples are shown in the following table.

★ Revision tip

If you choose not to perform an actual grade piece, or are doing a technology-based performance, you must ask your teacher for guidance as to the standard.

Area of study 1: Musical forms and devices

- A piece that makes a feature of a compositional device, e.g. sequence, imitation, arpeggio, 2-, 3- or 4-part textures, melody and accompaniment, etc.
- A piece written in a set form, e.g. binary, ternary, rondo, variation or strophic forms
- A piece written during the Western Classical Tradition, e.g. Baroque, Classical, Romantic

Area of Study 2: Music for ensemble

- Any piece from the chamber music tradition, e.g. a trio, duet, quartet (up to octet) taken from the Western Classical Tradition
- An ensemble that is an arrangement of any music linked with musical theatre
- Any musical arrangement that reflects jazz and/or blues genres

Area of Study 3: Film music

- A performance of any music used in a film, e.g. a song or arrangement of any piece linked with a film
- A suitable arrangement of any music that has been composed specifically for a film

Area of Study 4: Popular music

- Any group piece from any genre of popular music, e.g. rock, soul, reggae, pop ballad, hip-hop, etc.

Where can I find suitable pieces?

Solo

- ✓ Associated Board of the Royal School of Music (ABRSM)
- ✓ Trinity College London
- ✓ Trinity College Rock and Pop
- ✓ Rock School
- ✓ Vocal 'pop' solos

Ensemble

- ✓ Trinity College Rock and Pop
- ✓ Rock School (Grades 3, 5 and 8 for electric guitar, bass and kit)
- ✓ Rock Your School Music (Rhinegold Education)
- ✓ Vocal pieces (with added harmonies)
- ✓ ABRSM Music Medals (e.g. 'Keyboards Together')

Start by thinking about what style and type of music you want to perform and then present a selection of pieces to your teacher. It is a good idea to present three pieces: the one you would prefer to perform, a simpler piece – in case the first is considered too challenging for you – and a third for backup – in case the first two are both unsuitable.

Select a piece that shows your talents well – a piece which has variety, and as such allows you to demonstrate your practical ability. Experience has shown that students achieve a higher standard when they perform a piece that they know very well rather than a new piece they are still struggling

✅ Get the Grade

It is far better to perform a piece for which a score is available. If you have to make your own lead sheet then it must be detailed and include as much musical information as possible. That is the only way an assessor can judge the 'accuracy' of your performance.

 Remember

Vocal performances can include rapping, MC-ing and beat-boxing. If one of these is your particular interest, then work to impress. Consider your diction, and how to use your voice, breathing and any vocal effects to show control of the content, including the rhythmic patterns.

Revision tip

Use a metronome to keep the beat.

to come to terms with. When you are comfortable with the notes (pitch and rhythm) and have mastered the technical skill involved, then you can concentrate on the expression and interpretation in order to deliver a more impressive musical performance.

Look online for beat-boxing and rapping tutorials or documentaries which may be of interest and help to you. There are many that can be found on YouTube, for example.

Performing your own composition

This is something that may be of interest to some students, particularly those singer-songwriters who accompany themselves on the piano or guitar.

Choose only if it is the best option for you, and if it allows you to demonstrate your performing skills at the highest level you can.

Ensemble

In the ensemble examination everyone **must** perform as part of an ensemble. You can present all your pieces as ensembles if it suits you.

The ensemble:

- must consist of between two and eight performers
- should not resemble a solo with accompaniment
- must involve you performing-playing a part that is not doubled.

Important

If the piece sounds like a solo with accompaniment, then it is not considered to be a suitable ensemble piece. Choose something else.

Remember

Doubling occurs when someone is playing the same part as you.

Try playing or singing a few scales together before you start the rehearsal or performance.

Are you performing live with between one to seven other people?

Are all members of the group available for rehearsals?

Is your part of a suitable standard?

Consider

Each player should warm-up/tune individually.

A rehearsal is not a practice – all parts must be learnt prior to the rehearsal.

Ensure that your part allows you to perform the best you can.

The ensemble must last at least a minute.

Make sure that your part is not doubled in the ensemble.

Important

The other people in your ensemble do not need to be doing the GCSE Music examination. However, if they all come from your music class, you can rehearse in lesson time (if your teacher allows you to).

 Get the Grade

A few more marks are available if you can manage more difficult music fluently and successfully.

Checklist

- Are all the parts being performed accurately?
- Are the parts all well balanced? Is anyone drowned out?
- Does the piece last at least a minute?

It may be worth checking that your choice of music for the ensemble is appropriate for the assessment. Consider the following advice which has been issued by the exam board – it is a very useful guide.

Remember

- Make sure the piece is a good choice for you. Check with your class teacher.
- Record your work and listen to the recording. As a group, identify what needs to be done to bring about any improvement.

Is your piece suitable for an ensemble performance at GCSE?

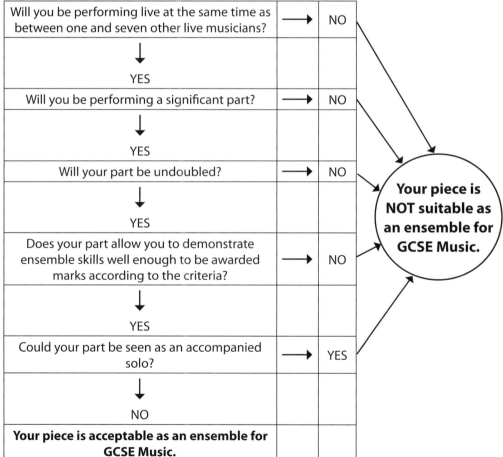

Will you be performing live at the same time as between one and seven other live musicians?	→	NO
↓ YES		
Will you be performing a significant part?	→	NO
↓ YES		
Will your part be undoubled?	→	NO
↓ YES		
Does your part allow you to demonstrate ensemble skills well enough to be awarded marks according to the criteria?	→	NO
↓ YES		
Could your part be seen as an accompanied solo?	→	YES
↓ NO		
Your piece is acceptable as an ensemble for GCSE Music.		

Your piece is NOT suitable as an ensemble for GCSE Music.

 Get the Grade

You are not restricted to just one instrument or voice, but there's no extra credit for showing the assessor that you are versatile and can play more than one instrument, or can sing as well as play. If you are the same standard on a number of instruments, then that's fine; actually, most students are better and more confident on one instrument (or voice) – and for the assessment that's what you should choose to do. Perform whichever way gets you the most marks.

Solo

You may choose to perform a solo piece. It may be accompanied or unaccompanied, but it is worth remembering that if an accompaniment exists you should perform the piece as the composer intended.

An accompaniment will give extra support and help in matters of tuning. Practise as often as you can with the accompanist, in front of others. Of course, you can use a pre-recorded backing track if you wish, and this is perfectly acceptable. You could also accompany yourself – if this is how you usually perform, and you are able to do this comfortably and confidently.

Improvisation

This is the art of creating music 'on the spot', i.e. performing and composing at the same time. You can prepare the improvisation in advance of the recording, and your response must be prepared to a stimulus. It is quite a challenging task but suitable for students who have a good ear, and are able to create musical ideas quickly and convincingly. For good marks, your performance must make musical sense and must be 'fluent'.

Some students enjoy improvising with melodic ideas. Others will prefer to work using a chord progression to guide their ideas. Go by ear – or by chords? The best scenario is probably a mixture of both.

⭐ Revision tip

Fluency means that you perform without hesitation or stopping due to errors in the performance.

💡 Remember

A copy of the stimulus must be given to the assessor.

What could I use as a stimulus?

Some suggestions for you to consider:

Chord sequences (various examples)	**Scales** (with examples on C)
D A Bm G	Any major scale, e.g. — C D E F G A B C
C G/D C/E F G F/A G/B C (ascending bass line)	Any minor scale, e.g. — C D Eb F G Ab B C
	Major pentatonic scale, e.g. — C D E G A
C G/B Am Am/G F C/E Dm7 C (descending bass line)	Minor pentatonic scale, e.g. — C Eb F G Bb
C G/B Am F Fm C	Blues scale, e.g. — C Eb F Gb G Bb C
Dm7 G7 Cmaj7 Fmaj7 Bm7(♭5) E7 Am7	Major/minor jazz modes, e.g. (Aeolian) — C D Eb F G Ab Bb
B♭C7 Cmin7 F7 B♭	Be-bop scale, e.g. — C D E F G Ab A B C
Typical 12-bar blues progression	(C major be-bop scale)

D7 (I)	G7 (IV)	D7 (I)	D7 (I)
G7 (IV)	G7 (IV)	D7 (I)	D7 (I)
A7 (V)	G7 (IV)	D7 (I)	A7 (V)*

*Finish the improvisation on D (I)

💡 Remember

If you are a drummer, you can improvise on a rhythmic pattern.

Technology

If you like DJ-ing or sequencing, this option may be right for you. Your teacher will be able to advise you on what sort of thing is suitable. Here too, you must provide a lead sheet for the assessor explaining all the relevant musical details including rhythm, tempo and performance directions (as well as details of any backing tracks). As with all other options, you must show an understanding of the style, and achieve musical balance and effective communication through manipulation of the sound sources, tone quality, effects and amplification.

DJ-ing

- You will need to demonstrate a combination of technical skills such as beat-matching, scratching, fading, beat-mixing/juggling, use of the cross-fader, turntablism, EQ and FX.
- You can use any equipment that you are familiar and comfortable with, including CDs and a laptop.
- Make sure that the lead sheet presents the necessary musical information. This could be presented within a table that shows the overall structure of your ideas.

Sequencing

- You should choose a suitable instrumental track or song, and sequence the parts into the computer to create a backing track. For a higher mark, think about creating at least three parts in order to present sufficient content.
- You must then perform one part 'live' for your performing assessment.
- For a group assessment (the ensemble) you must perform 'live' with another performer, against the sequenced backing track.
- You will need to demonstrate use and control of FX and quantise, include all performance effects, and present the musical material in the form of a table that follows the outline structure of the music.
- Show that you have the necessary practical skills to perform the 'live' part.

Know what is being assessed

Accuracy:

- Are the notes and rhythms correct?
- Is the performance fluent?
- Is an appropriate tempo maintained throughout?
- Are all the performance directions followed correctly?

Technical control

- Is the instrumental/vocal technique secure throughout?
- Is the tone well-controlled?
- Are the contrasts appropriate to the music?
- Is the performance well-projected?

Expression and interpretation

- Is the performance expressive?

- Is the performance stylistic?

- Is the music effectively communicated to the audience?

- Is the performance in the ensemble balanced and showing rapport between all performers?

- Where appropriate, is the balance between live and pre-recorded tracks effective?

Recording and assessment

You must perform your work in front of your music teacher, who will assess your performances and authenticate your work.

On the plus side ...

- You can perform and record your pieces at any time during the academic year in which you will take your assessment.

- You do not have to perform all the pieces on the same day.

- You can re-do the performance if you think you can improve it – but each attempt must be a performance of the whole piece.

How can I prepare for the practical assessment?				
Practise, practise, practise Set yourself deadlines and keep them	Always note your teacher's advice and suggestions for improvement	Plan ahead – don't leave things until the last minute	Gain experience of performing in front of an audience – family, friends, classmates, in school. This will give you added confidence	If possible, listen to some 'professional' recordings of your chosen pieces
Once you have mastered the notes and rhythms, pay attention to the performance directions in the music	Work for an accurate performance of your pieces	Sort out a practice schedule and stick to it Little and often is best	Get used to playing/singing your pieces through without stopping	Tune up before you perform Ensemble – play some scales altogether before starting, to check the tuning is consistent across instruments
Record yourself performing – moderate each others' work	Pianists – try the piano you will use for the assessment so you get used to playing it	Initially, practise sections of the piece – then join together, to achieve a fluent performance it in its entirety	Use a metronome if it helps during the practice	Check the timing of your pieces – does it all add up to four minutes?
Arrange plenty of rehearsals with your accompanist	Identify and correct problems such as wrong notes, hand positions, breathing, use of the pedal, etc.	Concentrate on the tricky passages to perfect them Be patient – practice makes perfect	Make sure your music is ready and all in order before the actual assessment, i.e. scores/lead sheets/backing tracks No last-minute panic	Warm-up beforehand Play or sing some scales or short exercises

Recording your performances

There's nothing wrong with feeling a little nervous before recording your pieces. Don't worry – sometimes this is a good thing. Your teacher understands what you are going through, and will give you a few minutes to settle yourself and prepare everything. The recording may be conducted as a conventional exam, or be completed during a lesson or lunchtime; where and when does not matter, as long as the recording is of good quality and the teacher is there with you.

Keep positive, and try to keep going if you make a mistake. This is your chance to show off.

Direct your nervous energy into the performance – this often heightens your awareness and your focus. Remind yourself that you know the music and know it well, and keep calm, control your breathing and concentrate on the music.

If all the hard work has been done beforehand, you will enjoy what you play.

WJEC – writing a programme note

BOOK LINK:
pages 226–229

Students following the WJEC course in Wales must present a programme note for the piece that has been connected to an area of study.

Remember

Things to remember about your programme note:

- It must be between 500 and 1,000 words.
- It must be entirely your own work, with teacher guidance and support.
- It does not need to be completed in class.
- Your teacher must see one draft, but only general feedback will be given (i.e. no formal written feedback).
- The quality of written communication **is assessed**, so you need to check your work very carefully.

There are clear guidelines for what you need to include in the programme note. You will need to research the piece, finding out a little about the background and the composer.

The following plan may prove useful as a guideline on what to include.

Section 1

✓ Include the name and dates of the composer, and what type of music they were famous for composing.

✓ When was the piece written?

✓ Details of the first performance.

✓ Explain how the piece links with the relevant area of study (include any additional points of interest that may be relevant).

Section 2

✓ Choose three or four of the prominent musical elements, and explain in **detail** their use in the piece. You could begin by describing the overall structure of the piece, giving the bar numbers of the sections. For example:

- Section A (bars 1–16)
- Section B (bars 17–32)
- Section A repeated (bars 33–48)

Some suggestions:

MELODY – You could explain the:

- structure of the theme
- phrase structure
- use of conjunct movement
- use of disjunct movement and intervals
- how the tune is varied or contrasted (pitch-shifting if appropriate).

RHYTHM – You could describe the:

- time signature (and what that means)
- what note-values are used
- features of particular interest (e.g. complex patterns, triplets, syncopation, dotted rhythms, beat-mixing as appropriate).

HARMONY – You could include details on:

- the key of the piece and any modulations (i.e. changes of key)
- the types of harmony overall (i.e. diatonic, chromatic, dissonant)
- the types of chords used (7ths, inversions)
- any significant chord progressions (including cadences)
- any features of particular interest (e.g. use of modes, the blues scale or 'blue' notes, the pentatonic scale, etc.).

TEXTURE – You could describe the:

- main texture (e.g. homophonic, melody plus accompaniment)
- interesting ways which may have been used to vary the texture (e.g. imitation, call and response, close vocal harmonies, use of layering, any 2-, 3- or 4-part textures, unison, countermelodies, canon, etc.)
- use of effects (music technology).

Section 3

Consider the technical performance demands of the piece.

This will include explanation of any challenges presented in terms of:

✓ the tempo

✓ dynamics and any variations of dynamics

✓ breath control (if appropriate)

✓ complex musical sections (tricky rhythms, difficult technical passages, a cappella sections)

✓ executing the performance directions and articulation in the music (bowing, use of legato or staccato in the piece, accented notes, phrasing, double stopping, glissandi, etc.)

✓ balance between parts (including the accompaniment).

 **Revision tip**

- Do not include an evaluation of the way you performed the piece.
- Carefully check your work for accurate grammar, punctuation and spelling.

CHAPTER 1

Activity 1.1

A1 Highest – note 5 (G); lowest – note 1 (A); middle – note 3 (D)

A2 Highest – note 1 (E♭); lowest – note 4 (F); middle – note 3 (C)

A3 Highest – note 2 (D#); lowest – note 1 (A); middle – note 4 (G)

A4 Highest – note 5 (F); lowest – note 1 (D); middle – note 3 (E♭)

A5 Highest – note 3 (F); lowest – note 2 (E); middle – note 4 (B)

A6 Highest – note 5 (D); lowest – note 2 (E); middle – note 4 (E)

A7 Highest – note 5 (G); lowest – note 4 (D); middle – note 1 (F)

A8 Highest – note 5 (F); lowest – note 2 (A); middle – note 3 (E♭)

A9 Highest – note 2 (D); lowest – note 4 (E); middle – note 1 (B)

A10 Highest – note 5 (A); lowest – note 3 (F); middle – note 1 (G)

A11 Highest – note 2 (E); lowest – note 1 (E); middle – note 4 (G)

A12 Highest – note 5 (F#); lowest – note 4 (B); middle – note 1 (D)

B1 Highest – note 2; lowest – note 4

B2 Highest – note 3; lowest – note 1

B3 Highest – note 4; lowest – note 2

B4 Highest – note 1; lowest – note 3

B5 Highest – note 2; lowest – note 3

B6 Highest – note 3; lowest – note 2

B7 Highest – note 4; lowest – note 3

B8 Highest – note 4; lowest – note 1

B9 Highest – note 1; lowest – note 4

B10 Highest – note 3; lowest – note 4

C1 Beethoven

C2 Tchaikovsky

C3 Mendelssohn

Activity 1.2

A1 Shortest – note 2 (quaver); longest – note 3 (minim)

A2 Shortest – note 2 (crotchet); longest – note 1 (dotted minim)

A3 Shortest – note 3 (quaver); longest – note 2 (dotted crotchet)

A4 Shortest – note 3 (semiquaver); longest – note 1 (minim)

A5 Shortest – note 1 (crotchet); longest – note 2 (minim)

A6 Shortest – note 2 (crotchet); longest – note 1 (semibreve)

B1 Simple time (2/4 – vivace)

B2 Simple time (3/4 – moderato e grazioso)

B3 Compound time (6/8 – allegro moderato)

B4 Simple time (4/4 – andante)

B5 Compound time (6/8 – allegretto pastorale)

D1 Option 2

D2 Option 2

D3 Option 1

Activity 1.3

A1 Disjunct (major)

A2 Conjunct (major)

A3 Disjunct (major)

A4 Conjunct (minor)

B1 Anacrusis, mix of conjunct and disjunct movement

B2 Sequence, chromatic movement

B3 Conjunct movement, fanfare style, use of tonic and dominant notes

B4 Arpeggio ideas, octave leap, trill

Activity 1.4

A1

Chord 1▶	Major	Chord 2▶	Minor
Chord 3▶	Major	Chord 4▶	Minor
Chord 5▶	Minor	Chord 6▶	Major
Chord 7▶	Minor	Chord 8▶	Major
Chord 9▶	Major	Chord 10▶	Major

B Extract 1 – Diatonic
Extract 2 – Dissonant
Extract 3 – Diatonic
Extract 4 – Chromatic
Extract 5 – Dissonant
Extract 6 – Chromatic

Activity 1.5

A

Extract 1▶	Pentatonic
Extract 2▶	Major
Extract 3▶	Pentatonic
Extract 4▶	Minor
Extract 5▶	Major

B Extract 1 – Minor key throughout
Extract 2 – Major key throughout
Extract 3 – Modulates minor ⇒ major
Extract 4 – Modulates major ⇒ minor

Activity 1.6

A

Binary form	A B
Strophic form	A B A B A B etc.
Rondo form	A B A C A
32-bar song form	A A B A
Ternary form	A B A

B1 False

B2 True

B3 False

B4 True

B5 False

B6 True

Activity 1.7

A1 The first note of bar 8

A2 The 4th note of bar 2

A3 From bar 5 (also bar 7)

A4 Bar 2 (also bar 8)

Activity 1.8

INSTRUMENTS

1 Piccolo

2 Piano, harpsichord, organ (+ synthesizer, etc.)

3 Oboe, cor anglais, bassoon

4 A mute is used to alter or 'colour' the sound. The pitch can be changed by the player changing the lip position, and using the valves (also the slide on a trombone).

5 Four: string, woodwind, brass, percussion

6 By blowing across the hole in the mouthpiece (or head).

7 Because it has lots more strings, which are plucked – never played with a bow.

8 When the strings are played without pressing the fingers on the fingerboard.

9 Usually 4 (5 and 6 string also sometimes used)

10 A wind band normally consists of mainly woodwind instruments (sometimes with added percussion); an orchestra consists of strings, brass, woodwind and percussion.

11 String quartet

12 When the strings on a string instrument are plucked.

13 Tuned percussion instruments can play different note pitches; untuned ones can't.

14 Timpani

15 A drum stroke in which the stick strikes the rim and head of the drum at the same time.

VOICES

1 Soprano

2 Bass

3 Soprano, Alto, Tenor, Bass

4 The baritone range of voice is lower than the tenor range.

5 A soprano range is higher than the contralto (alto) range.

6 A mezzo-soprano is a voice range pitched between soprano and contralto.

7 A cappella

8 Humming

9 Falsetto

10 Rap

11 Melismatic

12 Scat singing

13 The chorus

14 Syllabic

15 Male voice choir

TECHNOLOGY

1 Musical Instrument Digital Interface

2 Synthesiser

3 Distortion/Overdrive

4 An effect where the sound produced by an amplifier is made to reverberate slightly.

5 A sampler is a bit like a synthesiser, but it uses sound recordings (or 'samples') of real instrument sounds (e.g. a piano, violin or trumpet), or excerpts from recorded songs (e.g. an actual recording)

6 True

7 False

8 This is a type of lever used with a guitar which adds **vibrato** to the sound by changing the tension of the strings (sometimes called a whammy bar)

9 A tremolo effect is a kind of 'stuttering' or ''pulsating' effect created on guitar, where the movement and rhythm is created by varying the amplitude or volume of the signal – found on many amps, and in certain stomp boxes. (Sometimes confused with vibrato, a technique that varies the pitch of the note very subtly.)

10 Panning; audio mixing

Activity 1.9

A1 Homophonic

A2 Polyphonic

A3 Monophonic

A4 Homophonic

A5 Monophonic

A6 Polyphonic

CHAPTER 2

Activity 2.1

1 major in first inversion

2 a dominant 7th in first inversion

3 a D major chord

4 a tonic chord

5 a submediant chord in root position

Activity 2.2

1 False, True, True, False, False, True, False

2 an imperfect cadence

3 D G A C

4 a tone then a 3rd

5

The only power chord used in this piece	is the chord of D5.
A chord written as D/F# means that	the second note is the one heard in the bass.
There is a modulation to D major	in the verse section of this song.
The first part of the bass line in the verse	uses a descending minim pattern.
The first part of the bridge section	includes a solo for the lead guitarist.
This piece begins with	a syncopated chordal idea.

5 The complete sentences are as follow:

The only minor chord used in this piece	is the chord of G minor.
A chord written as B♭/A♭ means that	the second note is the one heard in the bass.
One bar in this song	has a different time-signature than the rest.
The first part of the bass line in the outro	uses a dotted rhythm pattern.
The last bar of the piece	includes an upwards suspension.
This piece begins with	a descending minim idea in the bass.

CHAPTER 3

Activity 3.1

1 minor in 1st inversion

2 a dominant in root position

3 an A major chord

4 the tonic minor 7th in 3rd inversion

5 a submediant chord in 1st inversion

Activity 3.2

1 False, True, False, True, False, False, True

2 a perfect cadence

3 F G B♭ E♭

4 a 5th followed by a 4th

CHAPTER 4

Activity 4.4

1 (a) Option 3; 3/4; C major

   (b) Option 2; 2/4; D minor

   (c) Option 1; 4/4; E♭ major

   (d) Option 2; 6/8; A major

   (e) Option 1; 4/4; A♭ major

   (f) Option 3; 6/8; E minor

   (g) Option 1; 2/4; B♭ major

   (h) Option 1; 4/4; C# minor

Activity 4.4

2 (a) Tonality: major

(b) Tonality: minor

(c) Tonality: major

(d) Tonality: major

(e) Tonality: minor

(f) Tonality: major

(g) Tonality: major

(h) Tonality: minor

3 (a) Key: A major

(b) Key: F major

(c) Key: E major

(d) Key: D major

(e) Key: C major

(f) Key: G major

(g) Key: B♭ major

(h) Key: A♭ major

4 (a) Key: C major

(b) Key: G major

(c) Key: F major

(d) Key: B♭ major

(e) Key: E major

(f) Key: E♭ major

(g) Key: A major

(h) Key: D major

Cadence in bar 2 is imperfect. Cadence in bar 4 is perfect.

5 (a) Key: E minor; compound duple

(b) Key: C# minor; simple triple

(c) Key: D minor; simple duple

(d) Key: A minor; simple quadruple

(e) Key: C minor; compound duple

(f) Key: F# minor; simple duple

(g) Key: A minor; simple triple

(h) Key: F minor; simple quadruple

(i) Key: G minor; compound duple

(j) Key: B minor; simple triple

6 (i) Plagal; major

(ii) Perfect; minor

(iii) Imperfect; major

(iv) Plagal; minor

(v) Imperfect; minor

(vi) Interrupted; major

(vii) Perfect; major

(viii) Imperfect; major

(ix) Interrupted; major

(x) Imperfect; minor

CHAPTER 5

Activity 5.1

Below are some suggestions of points which may be included in the answer. The list is not exhaustive, but typical of observations made by strong GCSE Music candidates.

Musical elements:

- Structure: Opening fanfare – main theme (played twice), third repeat shifts to short choral section, start of guitar improvisation. Distinctive, theme which establishes the strong character.
- Rhythm: 4/4 (simple quadruple), triplet rhythms in the fanfare idea, driving steady rhythms played by drums, quite simple note values (main motif in the introduction is one quaver, two semiquaver pattern), steady and regular beat throughout the extract. This give a sense of power and determination.
- Dynamics: Forte, maintained throughout, moving to ff in the choral section. This builds and reinforces the sense of excitement.
- Melody: Opening fanfare based on triadic idea and shape, use of repeated notes with the triplet patterns, theme has strong opening motif of three notes (semiquaver ⇒ dotted quaver, dotted minim; two quavers dotted minim acceptable). End of melody persists with a repeated note on one pitch, note the constant use of patterns, opening motif developed by choir, range is widened when the beginning of the choral section starts an 8ve higher than previously, freer melodic content with improvisation in guitar at end of extract, etc. These new ideas add further animation and a sense of anticipation – the repeated note may be taken as the relentless 'punching' of the boxer in training.
- Harmony: Diatonic, major key, opening fanfare built on notes of the tonic chord, idea ends on V ready for theme in the tonic
- Texture: Homophonic, melody plus accompaniment
- Style and mood: Cinematic, rock, exciting; the music supports the feeling of challenge and adventure
- Instrumentation: Synthesised, orchestra + rock band, brass orientated (e.g. opening fanfare in trumpets), mixed choir provide vocals with a verse after the 2nd repeat of the main theme.

ANSWERS TO EXAM-STYLE QUESTIONS

Please note that these are suggested answers that would achieve a good mark if you gave them in an exam. They are designed to help guide and instruct you, but they should not be considered to be the only answers you could give.

CHAPTER 1

Bach, *Minuet in G*

(a) **(i)** Option 3 is the correct bass line

 (ii) Imperfect cadence

 (iii) Sequence

 (iv)

(b) G major

(c) Harpsichord

(d) Moderato

Film theme, *Laurence of Arabia*

(a) **(i)** Timpani

 (ii) Tambourine (also tom-tom)

(b) The answer must include information about the musical elements identified in the musical extract. For example, the following observation would gain you credit in this question.

- The extract has two identifiable sections – a fiery and strong opening, followed by a broader, more lyrical section. The mood of each section is very different and contrasting.
- **Section 1**. This is a fiery and strong opening which portrays a powerful mood. It is led by the percussion section which appears threatening. The opening rhythm (♫♫ ♩.) is played by the timpani drums as a solo. This striking rhythmic pattern is a very distinctive rhythm which is echoed throughout the first section – and the use of rests adds to the dramatic intent. It is extended on the third repeat as the tension builds by adding more layers – i.e. brass and woodwind. Their contribution is a musical phrase which is heard twice, with additional percussion instruments added (including the suspended cymbal). The melodic line is conjunct and this part includes rapid scalic motifs. Dynamics are forte, and the performance delivery includes accented notes.

The music is in 4/4 time (simple quadruple). The tonality feels minor. The opening rhythmic pattern is heard twice towards the end of the section, decrescendo.

The purpose and intention of this music is to create an exciting opening which will reflect the epic nature of the film, and the dramatic fiery nature of the Arabian battles.

- **Section 2**. This is a more lyrical section which is broader and more reflective. The thematic content is extremely memorable, delivered by the string section which is in direct contrast to the previous section. The theme is played by the violins. It is very expressive and played piano. It is still in 4/4 (simple quadruple) time, but the note-values are less complex and the rhythm more regular – mainly crotchets and quavers, with a triplet used sometimes on the last beat of the bar. The main theme is 4 bars long, and the opening idea uses a falling 4th. The first chord is major, but the following content is based on exotic flavours, possibly an Arabian-type scale which would reflect the setting.

- The purpose and intention of the music is this section feels more romantic in its message, possibly to reflect the main character and the love interest. This is an orchestral score, symphonic in type.

In a long answer question such as this, the examiner will consider your answer and award marks according to a marking grid. For top marks, you must present a perceptive answer that gives a detailed explanation of the musical features, including judgement about how the content is appropriate and effective in setting the mood and atmosphere. You must include accurate use of specialist vocabulary to impress, and present the information well.

Beatles, 'Yesterday'

(a) Version 1:

Statement	Tick (for true)
The introduction is played on a percussion instrument .	
The introduction is two bars long.	✓
This song is sung by a bass singer.	
A string accompaniment is added in verse two.	✓

(b) Version 2:
  (i) The beat is slower.
  (ii) It is performed a cappella (unaccompanied).
  (iii) There are more voices (with some different harmonies).

(c) Version 3:
  (i) New melodic material played at the beginning.
  (ii) The introduction is longer.
  (iii) No vocals – it is an instrumental piece.

(d) The instruments performing are 'cellos.

'O Chan Mere Makna'

(a) Unaccompanied
(b) Moderato
(c) 4/4
(d) Vocal introduction / Instrumental intro or instrumental chorus / Verse / Chorus for voices and instruments
(e) **(i)** Vocal shouts (such as Ay! Ay!)
  (ii) Use of the Punjabi language
  (iii) The rhythmic patterns of the dhol drums
(f) **(i)** Strong and heavy bass line
  (ii) Repetition of phrases and use of repetition
(g) Indian wedding

Welsh folk music

(a) Humming
(b) (i) Introduction (ii) Verse 1
(c) The correct melody is option 3
(d) Major
(e) Rubato
(f) **(i)** a cappella
  (ii) male voice choir
  (iii) homophonic

CHAPTER 2

Mozart

(a) The Trio
(b) (i) A major (ii) D major
(c)

Features	Bars
A dominant 7th chord	3^1, 3^3, 4^3, 8^3 11^3, etc.
A supertonic chord	$11^{1 \text{ and } 2}$

(d) The note is A (below middle C).
(e) Ascending at first; includes a dotted rhythm for the first time in the piece; mainly conjunct; uses a sequence in bars 21 ⇒ 22 which descends by a 3rd; has a high pitch but narrow range.
(f) Running quavers; slower crotchet pattern in bass/ sometimes two crotchets/crotchet rests interspersed; dotted crotchet – quaver feature in violin 1 evident.

Rainbow

(a) The bridge section

(b) **(i)** It is an instrumental section, no voices in the first part of the section.

(ii) The melody is played by solo lead guitar (not in voice).

(iii) It is a lower pitch (also, the dynamic is quieter).

(c) dotted crotchet; quaver rhythm; triplet crotchet rhythm

(d) **(i)** E minor **(ii)** octave

(e) D5; power chord

(f) Russ Ballard

(g) 1979

CHAPTER 3

Purcell

(a) Section C

(b) **(i)** A minor **(ii)** D minor

(c)

Features	Bars
A dominant 7th chord	Bar 26^5; accept 31^5, also 29^5
A diminished chord	Bar 31^1

(d) E (3rd above middle C)

(e) Typical answers would include:

- Some dotted rhythms for the first time in the movement.
- Apart from the interval of a 5th bar 28 (last note) 29 (first note), all the movement is stepwise – conjunct.
- Motifs from earlier sections evident and included, e.g. four quaver descending from bar 2; also is a slight development of bar 2.
- Bars 25–26 descending sequence/bars 29–30 ascending sequence.
- Use of repetition as the melodic idea from bar 25 is used in five out of the eight bars, with only slight adjustment in bar 27.
- Pitch range is relatively narrow (within a minor 9th, A–top B♭).

Stereophonics

(a) Final verse 3 + chorus

(b) **(i)** G minor **(ii)** B flat major

(c) Sustained organ/and sustained strings/guitar – finger-picking style/drums added back in with fill just before the refrain/brass with trumpet playing melody to start the outro/ends piano only.

(d) Introduction

(e) 1967

Exam-style question Eduqas

'House of the Rising Sun'

(a)

Statement	Tick (for true)
The bass guitar plays a scalic idea in the introduction.	
The lead guitar part in the introduction is based on a triplet rhythm pattern.	✓
A tambourine plays a continuous semiquaver pattern in the verse.	
The chords change on every two beats.	✓

(b) The answer should include relevant comment about **Version 2** which show clear **differences** to the original version up to a maximum of 4 marks, e.g.:

- Performed by a symphonic orchestra.
- Falls into two sections: longer **introduction** which establishes a completely different mood; starts with high-pitched strings, ascending idea in the harp above dissonant harmonies.
- The beat is irregular; mood is rather 'spooky'.
- Short 'bluesy'-type melodic idea played on muted trumpet.
- Sitar also plays a short motif to fill in texture.
- Timp roll and low brass and bass play tonic and dominant chords to lead into the **verse**.
- The tune of the 'House of the Rising Sun' is heard at a low pitch, played by lower strings (cellos). The texture homophonic and dense.
- Mood is dark and sombre.
- Some melodic decoration is evident in the melody with added motifs in horns (also 'bluesy' in style).

[The examiner will not accept correct observations which do not highlight the differences to the original version.]

(c) The answer should include relevant comment about **Version 3** which show clear **differences** to the original version up to a maximum of 4 marks, e.g.:

- Tempo is slower.
- All equal note-values (i.e. triplet quavers).
- Original accompaniment pattern has been changed rhythmically (now without semiquavers).
- Harmonies have been changed, made more interesting including some different notes.
- Chords have been arranged differently, including some different notes.

- Introduction stops on a strummed guitar chord ready for the verse.
- Verse – in a reggae style.
- Mood is more up-beat.
- Vocal style is more clipped and with Jamaican accent.
- Accompaniment also in typical reggae style, with strummed chords on the off-beat.
- Held notes played by organ.
- Some short improvised melodic ideas on piano.

(d) Orchestral concert/London Symphony Orchestra concert/Evening of Classic Rock Symphonies, etc.

(e) Minor

Exam-style question WJEC

'House of the Rising Sun'

(a)

Statement	Tick (for true)
The bass guitar plays a scalic idea in the introduction.	
The lead guitar part in the introduction is based on a triplet rhythm pattern.	✓
A tambourine plays a continuous semiquaver pattern in the verse.	
The chords change on every two beats.	✓

(b) Fusion

(c) Version 1

Instrumentation:

- Performed by a 'pop' group – drum kit, keyboard/synthesiser, bass guitar, lead guitar, vocalist.
- Introduction played by guitars only.
- Lead guitar plays arpeggio-type chordal accompaniment.
- Bass guitar plays single notes, which support the harmony.
- Vocalist enters with verse 1, accompanied by keys and drums.

Other features of interest:

- Melodic range is quite narrow (within the range of an octave), includes conjunct and disjunct movement.
- Harmony is diatonic.
- Rhythm is regular.
- Time signature is 6/8 – compound duple.
- Tonality is minor.
- Vocal is male – baritone.
- Texture is melody + accompaniment/homophonic.
- Structure of extract is two sections: introduction and verse.

Version 2

Instrumentation:

- Performed by a symphonic orchestra.
- Starts with high-pitched strings.
- Ascending idea in harp.
- 'Bluesy' idea in muted trumpet.
- Short motif in sitar.
- Timp roll and low brass/bass lead into the verse.
- Added motifs in horns.
- Theme of 'House of the Rising Sun' is played by lower strings (cellos).

Other features of interest:

- Longer **introduction** – new material.
- Establishes a completely different mood/now dark and sombre (rather 'spooky').
- Some dissonant harmonies heard in intro.
- The beat is irregular.
- New melodic material influenced by 'blues'.
- Theme is now a much lower pitch than Version 1.
- Melodic decoration evident in the melody.
- Texture is homophonic and dense, with more layers.

INDEX